Ships, Shoals and Amphoras

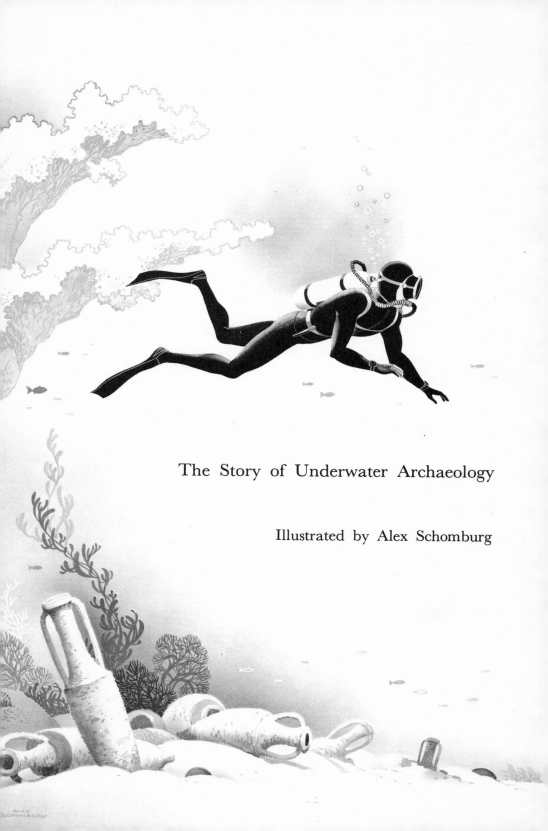

The Story of Underwater Archaeology

Illustrated by Alex Schomburg

SHIPS,
SHOALS
and
AMPHORAS

Suzanne de Borhegyi

Holt, Rinehart and Winston

New York • Chicago • San Francisco

Library of Congress Catalog Card Number: 61–9050

Designed by Ernst Reichl

ISBN: 0–03–036125–7

Printed in the United States of America

To Loni,

Stevie,

Carl, and

Christopher

Acknowledgments

I wish to express my very sincere appreciation to the many people who offered suggestions and contributed material for this book: to my mother and father, Mr. and Mrs. C. E. Sims, who read the manuscript and made many excellent contributions, both of an editorial and factual nature; and to Dr. Edgar End, who gave me much needed information on diving physiology. Thanks of a very special kind go to my husband, not only was he a great help because of his vast fund of knowledge of Old World and New World archaeology, but his encouragement and forbearance were of the utmost necessity in seeing this book to its completion.

Contents

Ships, Shoals and Amphoras

Foreword

"The time has come," the Walrus said,
"To talk of many things:
 Of ships and shoals and amphoras,
 And sunken gold of kings,
 And if there's treasure in a pot,
 And what the future brings."

 —*with apologies to Lewis Carroll*

In June, 1943, a French Navy captain named Jacques-Yves Cousteau reversed a billion years of evolution. With flexible, rubber foot fins, an airtight glass mask covering his eyes and nose, and two rubber hoses leading from his mouth to a set of three metal cylinders of compressed air on his back he looked like a weird creature from another world. Once in the water, however, he swam with the agility of a fish. A cycle was being completed. Man, who owed his origin to the sea, had returned to it. With the self-contained underwater-breathing apparatus he was free at last to explore and conquer the underwater world.

1

Through the Looking Glass

COME, put on your swim mask and fins and compressed-air tank and dive with us through the looking glass into the sea.

Down we go into the cool blue waters to a strange new world. Just as the image in a mirror is reversed, so life in the water is different from life on land. The water is a world without shadows and without an horizon. Of the 197,000,000 square miles of the earth's surface a little over seven-tenths is covered with water. Some parts are more densely populated than any area of comparable size on dry land, but there are also immense, trackless blue wastes that dwarf the greatest of earth's deserts.

Here we find animals that look like plants and are solidly rooted. We see plants that float about freely. There is no gravity. Our bodies are weightless. Our lungs take on a new function. Inhaling a great chestful of air we soar toward the surface. Exhaling we drift slowly downward. We sit, stand, lie back, and relax. A flick of our fins sends us gliding forward, as silently as the fish which watch us curiously in the murky distance.

The senses that we find so necessary for existence in our natural-air environment seem strangely inadequate. Our eyes deceive us and distort the size and nearness of things. Without our masks we would be almost blind. Diving to the bottom, thirty feet below, we find our ears to be more of a nuisance than a blessing. In them we feel the pressure of the water as a pain that can be relieved only by swallowing or blowing sharply through the nose. We strain our ears for a familiar sound, but around us is an eerie silence, broken only by the reassuring gurgle of exhaust bubbles from the regulator of our air tank.

Near us the sunshine from the upper world has made everything glow in a pure and luminous light, but at a distance of a few yards everything fades away in a blue haze. Below is a sandy floor strewn with rocks and seaweed, and until we come along it is absolutely motionless. Beyond us the bottom slopes away into the black abyss. Not until we are thoroughly accustomed to our new existence in this underwater world will we attempt to explore at greater depths. Even the most experienced divers find these depths cold and forbidding. At twenty fathoms (120 feet) we would discover a monochromatic world made up of an infinite number of shades of blue. Photoflash pictures have shown that vibrant color exists at this depth, but it cannot be seen, for the sea water acts as a filter, absorbing all but the blue rays of light. If we were to cut ourselves on a jagged piece of coral even our blood would look blue.

We could lose track of our directions and not know which way was up, but a cool head would tell us to follow the direction of our air bubbles. No, the depths are not for wandering. In time we will explore their mysteries, but for the moment we are quite content to soar up and back to the sunlight.

Above us we see the thrashing arms and legs of a swimmer. How tiring his exertions seem to us now! We pity him, and delight in our own freedom and ease of movement. We actually feel more akin to the fish around us than to this churning, splashing foreigner from dry land. With a bit of a shock we realize that we have gone through a metamorphosis. With the self-contained breathing apparatus we have temporarily become amphibians.

In order to differentiate between the three forms of underwater diving new terms have had to be devised. *Skin-diving* is the proper term for divers who use no breathing equipment. Their time under water is limited to the expiration of one chestful of air. *Helmet-diving* refers to divers who use the traditional diving suit with its weighted boots, metal helmet, life line, and air line connecting them with the surface. The diver who uses any kind of self-contained breathing apparatus is known as a *Scuba diver*. The term "Scuba" is an abbreviation of self-contained, underwater-breathing apparatus.

Man has gladly and eagerly accepted the challenge of the deep. Each year more and more men and women join the ranks of Scuba divers. However, the ease with which one learns to swim with breathing equipment is deceptive. The underwater world is not without its dangers. No one but a competent swimmer should attempt to dive. Even then, a complete course in the use of underwater-breathing equipment is an absolute necessity. Those who are qualified must be constantly on guard for the unexpected. In the water it is fear, panic, and fool-hardiness that are the most likely killers. And, of course, no one should ever dive alone. Understanding and accepting these limitations must be the first step in conquering the deep.

Once we train ourselves to pass with ease through the watery looking glass we find a new world waiting to be discovered. We feel the thrill of adventure that comes with the sense of exploring the unknown. The sea has its sinister aspects but it can also be exquisitely beautiful. It offers rare opportunities for sport and scientific exploration. It also hides many of the secrets of man's past.

For as long as man has lived on earth he has made good use of its many rivers, lakes, and seas. He drank the water; ate the fish and shellfish; and adorned himself with pearls, coral, and shells. He found it easier to travel by boat along a water route than to cross deserts, swamps, and mountains. At different times and places he even imagined the waters to be populated with gods, and he worshiped them. Whenever he lived on or near the shore he left clues to his past in the water. Archaeologists—men who study man's ancient, unwritten history—have long been aware of this. It is not surprising that with the invention of various kinds of underwater-breathing apparatus has come a new method of investigating the history of man: underwater archaeology. The science is young, but in its short life it has caught the imagination of scores of divers.

There is still air in our tanks. Come, and we will show you something else. We are swimming off the Côte d'Azur, the blue coast of southern France. Here at Anthéor, not far from Cannes, on a summer's day in 1948 a most interesting discovery was made quite by accident. Henri Broussard, one of the French pioneers of Scuba-diving and founder of the famous Club Alpin Sous Marin (Underwater Mountain Climbing Club) of Cannes, was swimming in leisurely fashion along the sea floor, enjoying the beauty of these waters, when he chanced to put his hand on an object hidden beneath the weeds. It turned out to be an amphora, the graceful earthenware storage jar of the ancient Greeks and Romans. His interest was aroused immediately and he began to explore the area carefully, foot by foot. To his surprise he found that there was not only one amphora but hundreds of them. From previous experience he knew this to be a sure sign of an ancient shipwreck. Many dives later he concluded that there were three separate wrecks. The outline of one ship was visible. Broussard took measurements and found that it was about a hundred feet long. Some of the amphoras discovered were the short, stubby kind that were used to store and transport olive oil during the second century before Christ. Others were tall and slim, and had been used for carrying and storing wine during the first century B.C.

A year later an amphora was found with its stopper still in place. What was more remarkable, the stopper had an inscription. This inscription was written in the Oscan alphabet, a language used by one of the original tribes of central Italy and which was spoken in the provinces long after Latin became the official language of Rome. For a long time the inscription defied interpretation. The credit for successfully deciphering the names of a certain Marcus and a certain Caius Lassius goes to a French scientist, Monsieur Jacques Heurgon. Armed with this information he checked many an ancient document until he found the name of Lassius among the funerary inscriptions on tombstones at the ancient town of Pompeii in southern Italy. The stopper of the wine jar had apparently been stamped with the name of the wineseller, and indeed records showed that the Lassius family were rich vine-growers and export merchants. They cultivated the famous vineyards that covered the lower slopes of Mount Vesuvius. The stopper itself was made of a porous volcanic rock characteristic of Mount Vesuvius. Both the style of the amphora and the records from Pompeii gave the date of one of the Anthéor wrecks at somewhere around 80 B.C. This is the story told by the wine jars.

One day, about two thousand years ago, two merchants from the town of Pompeii, by name Marcus and Caius Lassius, saw their wine jars loaded on a huge ship. The vessel was to carry the wine for sale to the Roman colonies on the coast of France. The Lassius family business was flourishing. As yet no grapes were grown in France, but according to the Roman historian Diodorus Siculus the ancient Gauls were enthusiastic drinkers. They happily paid the price of a slave for just one jar of sweet Italian wine.

The Lassius brothers watched the ship sail out of sight before returning to their vineyards. They may already have been thinking of ways to spend the fine profit from the sale of the wine. To their dismay, several weeks later they received word that the great ship had foundered on a treacherous reef and gone to the bottom with her entire cargo.

What is there to see today at the bottom? It is not deep, only sixty-five feet. All that is left is a field of broken bits of pottery. Not a single jar has been left intact.

As soon as word got out that an archaeological discovery had been made at Anthéor amateur divers rushed from all parts of the French Riviera, and with thoughtless enthusiasm carried off hundreds of souvenirs of their visit. One day in 1949 an American yacht anchored over the wrecks and the owner arranged a special show for his guests. He put the davits of his ship at the disposal of the divers swimming there, so that they could bring up heavy articles from the sea bottom. It was one of the jars brought up that day that contained the stopper with the inscription. If this jar had been carried off as a souvenir to be stored at last in someone's attic—like so many others—we might never have known anything about it. Fortunately it was turned over to an archaeologist.

The Anthéor wrecks may have had other stories to tell, but we will probably never know them. The clues have been almost completely destroyed, the evidence carried away as souvenirs.

Anyone may admire the graceful lines of an ancient wine jar, but it whispers its story only into the ears of the initiated. The archaeologists' conclusions are not wild guesses. They come as the result of years of patient study and exacting observations. But to learn more about the science of underwater archaeology and the discoveries made below the waters of oceans, seas, and lakes, we will have to return to dry land.

2

Appointment with the Sea

THE Mediterranean is a smiling, gentle sea. Its waters are warm and clear. It has been called the "cradle of civilization," because the first great cities grew up along or near its shores. These cities were eager to trade their ideas and products. To the peoples of the Mediterranean the sea must have seemed an inviting highway, serving to unite them more than to separate them. Free of the many natural obstacles that made travel and transportation by land slow and dangerous, it is not surprising that it was the birthplace of shipping and of the art of navigation.

The Egyptians were probably the first people to build true ships. Their first vessels were large reed boats, which were made seaworthy by a waterproofing of pitch. The Bible quotes the prophet Isaiah as saying, "the land . . . which *is* beyond the rivers of Ethiopia: that sendeth ambassadors by the sea, even in vessels of bulrushes upon the waters . . ." Paintings and carvings in the tombs of early Egyptian pharaohs show that 4,500 years ago large wooden boats were built and propelled not only by many oarsmen but by the wind. According to some accounts these ships were as much as 180 feet in length and carried a crew of 120 men. About the year 1500 B.C. the first great queen known to history, Queen Hatshepsut of Egypt, sent out a fleet of merchant ships from her capital of Thebes. They traveled by way of the Red Sea as far as the Somali coast of Africa to bring back a huge cargo of incense and elephant ivory.

There is probably little truth to the belief that ancient sailors were afraid to sail out of sight of land. By the time Queen Hatshepsut was sending forth her ships to gather royal treasures there had already been established a commercial sea route between Egypt and the island of Crete. Cretan merchants made regular voyages between the two countries.

Crete owed all its might and wealth to the sea. The men of Crete were industrious sailors and sea merchants. They made their rocky island off the southern coast of Greece the stepping stone between east and west. They dearly loved the sea, and knew its creatures so intimately that some of the most beautiful and naturalistic fish paintings of all time were made by them.

In addition to building fleets of ships that sailed the eastern Mediterranean from Asia Minor to Italy the Cretans were famous for their beautiful cities and great palaces. They were superb craftsmen and produced fine pottery and jewelry. Until 1400 B.C. the Cretans virtually ruled the Aegean Sea. Then suddenly and dramatically their civilization came to an end. The splendid palaces vanished into rubble. Archaeologists are still searching for an explanation for this catastrophe. What seems most likely is that armies of Greeks from the mainland invaded and conquered the island. The wealth and the glory of Crete were extinguished forever, but her traditions and skills, her knowledge and love of the sea were passed on to her successors, the Greeks and the Phoenicians.

The finest sailors of antiquity were, without any doubt, the Phoenicians. Their two largest cities were the ports of Tyre and Sidon at the extreme eastern end of the Mediterranean.

The Egyptians may have been the first astronomers, but it was the Phoenicians who made a discovery that brought the art of navigation to a new height. They studied the movements of the stars and observed that of all the twinkling specks of light one alone did not change with the seasons. Since it steadily and reliably pointed to the North Pole it was named Polaris or the North Star. With this star to guide them the Phoenician sailors were able to sail by night as well as by day. It was many years before their Mediterranean neighbors discovered the secret behind their amazing ability to navigate in the dark.

The Phoenicians were also merchants and colonizers. They established colonies throughout the Aegean Sea. Later they settled on the islands of Malta, Sardinia, and Sicily. They founded Carthage on the coast of North Africa, and about 1,100 years before the birth of Christ reached the strait of Gibraltar and named it the "Pillars of Hercules." Having arrived at the end of the known world they continued unhesitatingly into the unknown Atlantic. Soon their ships were fetching tin from as far away as Britain. Ivory, slaves, and gold were brought from Africa, and spices and frankincense from India. In exchange they traded coral to the nobles of China and Greek sponges to all the people of the Mediterranean. They also traded woolens, colored by a precious purple dye.

It was this dye that made the Phoenicians famous. It was so costly that only the wealthiest rulers could afford to wear robes of this color. As a result, purple became a sign of royalty. Even today, His Holiness the Pope wears robes of Tyrian purple. The dye came from the sea. It was extracted from the bodies of salt-water snails belonging to the genus *Murex*.

The Phoenicians were extremely jealous of their sea power. They guarded their secrets well. Rather than let an enemy capture one of their ships they deliberately sank it. As a result, no one knows exactly what other tricks of navigation they may have used or what secret instruments they possessed. It is believed that they invented many of the legends of sea monsters, beautiful but treacherous sirens, and deadly whirlpools. By so doing they hoped to frighten off competition. Of course, these stories also added to their fame as seamen, and gave them an excuse for raising the price of their services. Nevertheless, in time their power waned and they were defeated in a war with their neighbors, the Persians. The Persians in turn were defeated by the Greeks.

← EGYPTIAN
OARED SHIP
⟨ 1600 B.C. ⟩

PHOENICIAN →
MERCHANTMAN
⟨ 750 B.C. ⟩

← GREEK
MERCHANTMAN
⟨ 250 B.C. ⟩

ROMAN →
MERCHANT
SAILING SHIP
⟨ A.D. 200 ⟩

ALEX
SCHOMBURG

The Greeks were able sailors, but not so daring as the Phoenicians. Their navy originally was intended only to defend the mainland from attack by the Persians. However, as Greece prospered, its large cities, such as Athens and Corinth, became too big to be supported by the surrounding countryside. Greek ships were soon importing thousands of bushels of grain from Egypt and the Near East in exchange for Greek wine, olive oil, and painted pottery dishes and kitchenware.

The sea was always important to the Greeks. A look at the map will show that Greece is made up of hundreds of islands and peninsulas. The sea is literally everywhere within and around the country. The ancient Greek religion was full of undersea tales. The Greek god of the sea was Poseidon, although he is better known today by his Roman name, Neptune. Poseidon, holding aloft a trident, rode the seas in a chariot drawn by horses and surrounded by dolphins and mermaids. Aphrodite, the Greek goddess of love, was born from the sea on a scallop shell. The greatest of all legendary divers was the god Glaucus. According to Greek mythology he was originally a mortal who discovered one day a magical grass. Having eaten this grass he was able to walk beneath the waters for hours at a time. Eventually he was welcomed by the sea gods and became one of them.

The famed golden fleece of Greek mythology may also have come from the sea. Very likely it was the silky fibers spun by the pinna clam. This odd material was used by the early Greeks and Romans to weave quantities of a beautiful and durable "silken" fabric.

In the fifth century B.C., while Greece rose to power in the east, the independent Phoenician colony of Carthage became the great commercial empire of the western Mediterranean. Carthage watched carefully over its seaways, and any trespassing ship was sunk. Carthaginian ships sailed into the Atlantic and followed the European coast as far north as the Baltic Sea. In 470 B.C., under the great leader Hanno, they sailed south along the African shore to found a new colony on the gulf of Guinea.

Rome gained control of the Mediterranean by conquering first Carthage and then Greece. She used her navy to expand her empire until it included most of the western world, and to carry on extensive trade with her far-flung colonies. However, the Romans, for all their naval strength, were never particularly good sailors. The Roman merchant ships were impressive in size and cargo capacity, but they were clumsy and almost always overloaded. The many Roman wrecks found along the ancient trade routes suggest that ship casualties must have been enormous.

Roman ships seldom ventured beyond the "Pillars of Hercules." When they did, they showed an ignorance of ocean tides that would have been laughable to the Phoenicians. Even the well-educated Julius Caesar was not aware of the gravitational effect of the sun and moon on the waters of the Atlantic. As a result he nearly lost an important campaign. When his troops invaded Britain in 55 B.C. he beached his ships on the east coast of Kent. The next morning he was surprised and dismayed to find his fleet stranded high and dry. It had been swept far up on the beach by a twenty-foot spring tide followed by a strong wind.

For roughly five thousand years the peoples of the Mediterranean loved their sea. They came to know it very well. Although they respected its moods they did not fear it. They learned to use it in every way possible: for trade, warfare, and transportation. Its treasures were collected and it was included in their religion. The Romans claimed all the lands along its shores. They called it, with good reason, *mare nostrum,* our sea.

But eventually the powerful Roman Empire began to crumble. Split into an eastern and a western half, it was torn with inner conflicts. There was not much left of greatness by the time it was conquered by barbarians from the north. These invaders had never lived near the sea. They disliked and distrusted it. In the Dark Ages that followed, the cities of Europe turned their backs on the sea. Legends of dreadful sea monsters invented by the Phoenicians were revived. People huddled together in little communities in ignorance and superstition. Most of the science and art of the Greeks and Romans was lost. Few people could read and even fewer could write. The writings of ancient scientists, historians, and statesmen that had not been lost were guarded in the libraries of monasteries, but most of these "pagan" works were forbidden.

The people who lived along the coasts were given additional reason to fear the sea. From it came hordes of pirates to plunder their villages, kill their men, and kidnap their women and chil-

SEA LEGENDS OF THE DARK AGES

dren. The pirates in the Mediterranean came from North Africa. They were Moslem Arabs, who claimed the Mediterranean after the fall of Rome. Followers of the religious leader Mohammed, they were dedicated to the destruction of Christianity.

The North Atlantic and Baltic coasts were at the mercy of the Vikings. These fearless, sturdy, bearded men were excellent shipbuilders and expert seamen. They, too, discovered many secrets of navigation, and sailed hundreds of miles across the seas to colonize Iceland and later Greenland. It seems quite likely that they were the first white men to discover the American continent. The great Norse explorer Leif Ericson apparently reached the shores of Labrador and Newfoundland about 1000 A.D., preceding Columbus by almost five hundred years.

Not all of the great seafarers were Europeans. Far off in the Pacific the brown-skinned Polynesians were skilled and daring voyagers. They were even better navigators than the Vikings. From their base in Tahiti they sailed their outrigger canoes thousands of miles, as far north as Hawaii and as far south as New Zealand. Archaeologists are even beginning to suspect that some of the Polynesian travelers reached the western shores of Central and South America long before Columbus made his historic voyage to the "Indies."

In the meantime a change was gradually taking place in Europe. The period called the Renaissance, meaning rebirth, that followed the Dark Ages was exactly what its name implied. After nearly a thousand years European man threw off the cloak of fear and superstition and began to relearn and rediscover the knowledge and arts of Egypt, Greece, and Rome. At the same time he revived his interest in the sea. The old stories of sea monsters were challenged and eventually disputed. Trade routes were re-established and new ones were opened. From eastern scientists European man learned to use the astrolabe and sextant and the miraculous compass. With these instruments he regained confidence in his ability to sail beyond the horizon. So began the Age of Exploration.

The main events are well known. In 1492 Christopher Columbus discovered the New World, although at the time he did not realize the importance of his discovery. A few years later the Portuguese explorer Vasco da Gama made his way around Africa to India. He was followed by Magellan, who, sailing under the Spanish flag, decided to prove that the earth was a sphere by sailing around it. Although Magellan was killed in the Philippine Islands one of his officers by the name of Del Cano completed the round trip. Eventually England, then France, began to challenge Spanish sea supremacy. The British explorer, Sir Francis Drake, was in command of the English fleet when the Spanish Armada met destruction in the English Channel. These were the pioneers of ocean travel. Many others followed in their wake, but that is almost recent history. It is sufficient to say that man had kept his appointment with the sea. It remained for him to conquer its depths.

3

Conquest of the Depths

THERE is a legend that Alexander the Great was so entranced with the wonders of the underwater world that he descended in a diving bell for several days to watch the activities of the sea creatures. He saw a sea serpent, so the story goes, that was so long it took four days to pass before his observation chamber. Today we do not believe in sea serpents, and we question the ability of anyone, even the mighty Alexander, to stay underwater for such a long time in a diving bell. Still, it makes a good story and it would not be surprising to learn that Alexander, who supposedly cried when he had no more lands to conquer, might have had designs on the sea.

On February 15, 1954, the French naval engineer Pierre Willm and his companion, Lieutenant Commander Georges Huout, looked out of the window of the bathyscaphe, *F.N.R.S.-3,* and saw the bottom of the Atlantic Ocean at a depth of about two-and-a-half miles (13,284 feet). They saw no sea serpents, but they did see a large-headed six-foot shark and a sea anemone. The story connecting the ancient legend and the modern scientific miracle is the epic of man's conquest of the deep.

Actually the story begins long before Alexander. It goes back to the dawn of prehistory, when glaciers covered most of the northern hemisphere. Ice-Age man caught fish in shallow water with a simple two-pronged spear. Archaeologists have found these spears, together with fish bones, in the caves where ancient men lived. In the very earliest times fish were not an important part of his diet, however. He lived amidst a plentiful supply of big game, the large meat and fur-bearing animals that he painted on the walls of caves in southern France and Spain.

The real exploitation of the sea began at the end of the last Ice Age, about ten thousand years ago. As the glaciers began to melt and the climate became warmer many of the large animals, like the mammoth and the wooly rhinoceros, became extinct. Others, like the reindeer, followed the glaciers and the cold weather to the north, where they have lived ever since. Forests grew up to cover the ground and give protection to new kinds of animals, like the elk, the deer, and the wild pig. They were much harder to catch than the massive, slow-moving Ice-Age mammals. European man, who had not yet heard of that marvelous African invention the bow and arrow, found food hard to come by. As a result he took to living along the shores of lakes and seas, where he could fish and hunt for clams and oysters. We know that in many regions shellfish were his major source of food. Archaeologists have excavated huge piles of the discarded shells that marked his prehistoric "kitchens." It was about this time that man invented such useful items as the fish-hook, the canoe, the harpoon and line, nets, and fish traps.

We do not know when men first learned to swim and dive for shellfish. At first he must have found them in shallow water and in tidal pools. Nevertheless, to gather the oysters, clams, scallops, and other shellfish that he relished, he would have had to dive for them in deeper water, too.

Even when other types of food became more plentiful man continued to dive. He made the discovery that the sea was a source of beauty, as well as nourishment. Instead of discarding all of the shells he kept the largest and prettiest for use as containers and oil lamps. Later he strung them on cords for necklaces and bracelets. Within the rough gray oyster shell he found one of the loveliest of all gems, the pearl, and its iridescent matrix, mother-of-pearl. The finest salt-water pearls have always

NATIVE PEARL DIVER

come from the Persian Gulf, where they are found at depths of between thirty and sixty feet. Such a depth strains a naked diver to the limit of his physical endurance, and yet men dived for these pearl oysters at least forty centuries ago. At this time civilization was just beginning in the Near East.

In 1927 and 1928 the British archaeologist Sir Charles Leonard Woolley excavated the ruins of an ancient Sumerian city in Mesopotamia near the Persian Gulf. There, in the royal graves of Ur, he found an exceedingly valuable archaeological treasure. This was the so-called "Standard of Ur," a panel covered with a mosaic of figures in mother-of-pearl and mussel shell. From it Woolley was able to construct a picture of what life had been like in Ur nearly five thousand years ago.

The Sumerians were not the only ancient people to value pearls and mother-of-pearl. Carved ornaments made about 2500 B.C. were found during excavations of Sixth Dynasty

Egyptian tombs. Nor were pearls and shell the only gems ancient man sought in the sea. He admired red coral and considered it to have magical properties. The belief survives today in many parts of the world.

Man also discovered that strange sea animal, the sponge, and its many uses. And he found two tiny varieties of sea snail that when crushed gave him the highly valued purple dye that made the Phoenicians famous. In short, man dived down through the waters in search of food and found there a veritable treasure house. By returning regularly to harvest the sea floor he made the first great stride in his conquest of the underwater world.

The ancient divers of the Mediterranean and the Persian Gulf, like those in primitive regions today, dived without the aid of equipment of any kind. Apparently they were able to descend to depths of sixty feet and more. Possibly they weighted themselves with heavy stones in order to plummet to the bottom with no waste of precious time. Or they may have dived with empty lungs, exhaling sharply before beginning their dive and then kicking hard for the bottom, just as the Pacific Islanders do today. Their biggest problem was to hold their breath long enough to get to the bottom and do their job. To do this required a lifetime of training.

Today the most seasoned divers average between one-and-a-half and two minutes under water on one breath. However, some almost unbelievable records have been made and authenticated in recent years. In 1913 a Greek sponge diver descended to a depth of two hundred feet to tie a line on the lost anchor of an Italian battleship. Another diver is recorded as having held his breath for four minutes and forty-five seconds, but this was in shallow water without moving. In Japan women pearl divers descend many times a day to depths of 145 feet.

The second step in man's conquest of the deep came with the invention of various kinds of equipment, which increased the efficiency of his dive and his time under water. The date that goggles were first used is not certain. But long before glass was known divers made lenses of thin slices of tortoise shell, which when highly polished were transparent. Today the one absolutely indispensable item in diving is the watertight mask. There is a good reason why a type of eye covering was one of the first and most important of man's underwater inventions.

If you stand at the edge of a swimming pool you can see every detail on the bottom, even though the pool may be as much as ten or eleven feet deep. The moment you put your head under water, however, your vision is cut to one or two very blurred feet. This is because your eye is constructed for sight in a world of air. Light passing through water is refracted differently. Your vision is blurred because the images do not converge properly on the retina at the back of the eye. There must be an air space in front of your eyes before they can focus on an image. This can be accomplished either with watertight goggles or a mask. However, goggles had two main defects: More often than not the two lenses caused the diver to see double; they also collapsed painfully against the face under the pressure of a deep dive.

The idea behind today's masks, which consist of one large glass plate and cover the nose as well as the eyes, did not develop until the late 1930's. Then everyone interested in diving seemed to arrive at the idea simultaneously. The single glass plate eliminates the problem of double vision. The diver is able to equalize the pressure of the water during a deep dive by exhaling air into the mask. Even though the mask makes objects appear larger and nearer than they are it opens man's eyes to the wonders of the underwater world, by giving it the appearance and clarity of an immense aquarium.

Another object which has come to be closely associated with the modern skin diver is his rubber breathing tube or snorkle. The idea of the breathing tube occurs in nature. There is a type of fly which spends the first stage of its life, as a maggot, under water. It breathes by means of a tail-like projection that is nothing more nor less than a breathing tube. Elephants have also been observed "snorkling." Although it is difficult to imagine that these ponderous beasts can swim they have been seen completely submerged except for the trunk, which is held above water for breathing. The Greeks knew about elephants, and possibly got the idea of a breathing tube from watching them in the water. At any rate they made great use of breathing tubes, as did the Romans centuries later. Like many another invention it was developed as an aid to warfare.

Almost everyone has read of an exciting escape during which the hero hid from his enemies in shallow water by breathing through a reed. Reeds were probably the first breathing tubes. Not only did they enable the swimmer to hide from his enemies; they also enabled him to engage in one of the oldest and most effective of military tactics, the sneak attack. As early as the time of Alexander the Great swimmers carried messages into blockaded ports, destroyed enemy defenses, and bored holes in enemy ships. Occasionally they were met by enemy swimmers, and there are records of several early underwater battles.

The earliest known diving helmet made use of a breathing tube which was kept afloat by an attached inflated bladder. It was probably invented during the early sixteenth century A.D., but we have no record of whether it was ever used. Such a device would have been absolutely useless at depths of more than four or five feet. Below five feet the pressure is so great that air cannot be drawn down through the tube, nor the exhausted air blown out. Anyone doubting this fact might try experimenting in a swimming pool with a length of garden hose.

The snorkle used today is essentially the same as that used in ancient times, except that reed has been replaced by rubber. It is useful only for skimming along the surface, but it does permit the swimmer to keep his eyes under water and breathe at the same time.

The trademark of the modern skin diver are his rubber foot

fins. These clumsy-looking appendages were responsible for the term frogman, a name considered derogatory by most skin divers. These fins add about forty per cent more power to the foot stroke and make it possible for the diver to move easily without having to use his hands. Although not as old as the mask and snorkle, various versions of hand and foot fins were designed by such well-known historical personages as Leonardo da Vinci in the sixteenth century and Benjamin Franklin in the eighteenth century. The kind used today were first patented by the Frenchman Louis de Corlieu in 1933.

The ancients of the Mediterranean must be given credit for taking the third step toward conquering the deep. They were the first to experiment with methods of carrying a supply of air below the surface. The Greeks have been credited with inventing the diving bell. According to the Greek philosopher Aristotle, diving bells were used very successfully during Alexander the Great's siege of the Phoenician port of Tyre in 333 B.C. With them his swimmers were able to destroy underwater obstacles intended to prevent the Greek fleet from entering the harbor. These bells were also used by Greek sponge fishermen.

The principle of the diving bell is simplicity itself. Plunge a glass mouth down into a container of water and you will see that air is trapped inside the glass. The Greeks submerged huge pottery vases and suspended them from their ships or floats. The divers, at work under water, could pop up under the inverted cones as often as they needed for a fresh supply of air. The only way to replenish the air in the diving bell, however, was to haul the whole heavy contraption to the surface.

There was a gap of over two thousand years before an English astronomer, Sir Edmund Halley (better known for the comet which bears his name), finally invented a means of carrying air from the surface down to the diving bell. His innovation, which he patented in 1691, consisted of two thirty-six-gallon barrels filled with air and attached to the diving bell by an arrangement of counterweights and pulleys. Each barrel had an open hole in the bottom and an air hose extending from the top. So long as the air hose hung lower than the hole on the bottom, the water pressure prevented the air from escaping. To transfer air from the barrel to the inside of the bell the diver lifted the open end of the hose to the top of the bell and the air flowed in. The continuous raising and lowering of the barrels kept the divers supplied with fresh air.

The next step was to substitute a hose and pump for Halley's barrels. This was accomplished in 1771 by John Smeaton, an English civil engineer. Further improvements were made, until the simple device invented by the Greeks had become the huge caisson used today to excavate and lay the foundations for bridges, subways, and tunnels. The modern version of the diving bell is a large chamber into which compressed air is pumped. The men who work in these caissons are known as sandhogs. The strange sickness that attacked them became known as caisson disease or the bends. It will be discussed in greater detail in the following chapter. Edmund Halley can also be credited with the invention of the first functional diving helmet. It was a combination of a diving bell and helmet suit. The diver wore a wooden helmet, which was linked by a pipe to a submerged air-filled tub. However, the diver soon exhausted the air in the tub and had to come to the surface for a new supply. The breakthrough came in June, 1797, when the German scientist Otto Klingert constructed a tin helmet with pipes leading to the surface. For the first time air was forced down through the pipe to the mouthpiece of the helmet by a pair of bellows. In 1819 a German scientist working in England, Augustus Siebe, adapted Klingert's idea to a diving suit with a removable metal headpiece attached to a waterproof jacket. Compressed air entered the helmet by an intake valve. The excess air flowed down into the jacket and escaped around the waist. The trouble with this suit was that the diver could not bend over without getting water into his helmet. In 1837 Siebe solved the problem by inventing the closed diving suit, with both intake and outlet valves in the helmet. The idea was so successful that it became the model for all later helmet suits.

Those who have followed Captain Nemo's adventures in Jules Verne's classic *Twenty Thousand Leagues Under the Sea* usually credit the author with a rich but unscientific imagination. Actually the underwater-breathing apparatus that he described was far from imaginary. It was invented in 1863. The little-known inventors of the first semi-independent breathing apparatus, both contemporaries and countrymen of Jules Verne, were Benoit Rouquayrol, a mining engineer, and Lieutenant Auguste Denayrouze, an officer in the French navy. According to their design the diver carried a tank on his back, which was filled with air forced down through a pipe. It was quite possible for a diver using this contraption to detach the pump line and walk about freely, as long as the air supply in the tank held out. This device was introduced to the sponge divers of the Aegean in 1866. It was used with such success that it is surprising that it never became popular. The reason probably lies in the fact that the Siebe suit, invented earlier, had more and better publicity.

In 1879 an independent underwater-breathing apparatus was devised that used pure oxygen. Its inventor was an English merchant seaman by the name of Henry Fleuss. The diver carried a tank of oxygen on his back. This was connected to his rubber face mask by two breathing tubes. The air in the system was used over and over again. The exhaled air simply passed through a bag containing caustic potash which absorbed the waste carbon dioxide. It was replenished with oxygen and was again ready for use. A type of oxygen "rebreathing" unit was used with great success by United States, British, and Italian frogmen during World War II. Since no air escapes there is no telltale trail of bubbles on the surface. When divers began experimenting with this device at depths below thirty feet, however, they found that oxygen under pressure causes frightful convulsions and even death.

The direct ancestor of the modern compressed-air diving lung was invented by Commandant Yves Le Prieur of the French navy. In 1926 he and a countryman, Fernez, obtained a French patent for the Fernez-Le Prieur self-contained diving apparatus, and in 1933 Le Prieur brought out an improved and enlarged version of the original design. The bottle of compressed air was strapped on the side of the diver. The air, which passed through an air pipe to a full face mask, was released manually by means of a hand valve.

In 1943 Captain Jacques-Yves Cousteau hit upon a means of improving the Le Prieur apparatus. He asked the French engineer Emile Gagnan to devise a fully automatic regulator that would feed the proper amount of air to the diver regardless of his position. Gagnan made his regulator from a plastic valve, the kind used on the gas tanks of French wartime automobiles. Cousteau and Gagnan patented the device which became an integral part of the now famous Aqualung. With it man was really free for the first time to explore the underwater world.

Another one of the problems man faced in the water was that of keeping himself warm. This is because water, being a better conductor than air, quickly drains off body heat. The warm-blooded aquatic mammals are equipped by nature with an insulating layer of blubber. Man had to devise his own insulation.

Any form of body covering is a help, but the best protection is afforded by an exposure suit. These are of two types, wet and dry. The dry suit is made of thin rubber and must be watertight. Woolen clothing is usually worn underneath for additional warmth. The wet suit, made of foam neoprene, gets its name from the fact that a small amount of water enters the suit. This water is quickly warmed to body temperature. Since neoprene is an excellent insulator the diver is as comfortable as if he were swimming in a warm bath.

A completely different type of diving suit, invented in 1923, was made entirely of metal with movable arms and legs. It was strong enough to withstand the water pressure of moderate depths, with the result that the air pressure inside the suit could be the same as at the surface. It was a clumsy contraption and the diver's movements were limited, but in it a man could work as deep as three hundred feet for an hour or more and still ascend rapidly to the surface with no ill effects.

Exploration at even greater depths was begun by the American naturalist William Beebe. He designed a research ship called a bathysphere, which was a hollow steel ball able to endure tremendous pressure. It was suspended by a heavy steel cable from a ship on the surface. In it, in 1934, Beebe reached a depth of 3,028 feet off the coast of Bermuda. From his little observation window he viewed weird deep-sea creatures never before seen by man.

A more recent descent, that of the bathyscaphe, *F.N.R.S.-3*, was mentioned at the beginning of this chapter. Bathyscaphe means deep boat in Greek. The first bathyscaphe was de-

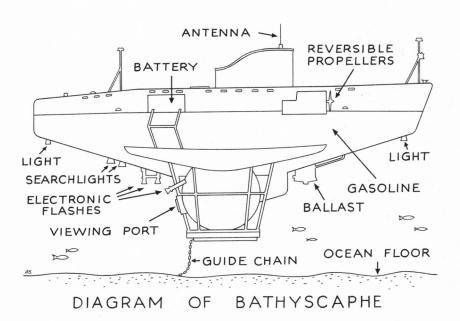

DIAGRAM OF BATHYSCAPHE

signed by the Swiss physicist, Auguste Piccard, who had earlier become famous by ascending in a balloon to a height of 53,152 feet. In fact the bathyscaphe operates on the same principle as a balloon: It is completely independent of the surface, having no cable line.

Gas in a balloon makes it lighter than air. Bags of sand were carried during early balloon ascensions to weight the balloon and control its rate of ascent. To make the balloon rise some of the sand was thrown overboard. In order to descend gas was released from the balloon, making it less buoyant.

It is a high-grade gasoline carried in a large tank above the observation chamber that makes the bathyscaphe much lighter than water. Iron shot held to the bottom of the bathyscaphe by a powerful electromagnet gives it weight. All that is necessary to make the depth ship rise once again to the surface is to release the load of iron shot.

In January, 1960, another bathyscaphe, the *Trieste,* with Dr. Piccard and United States Navy Lieutenant Don Walsh aboard, plunged 35,640 feet (five miles) into the Marianas trench near Guam.

Jacques-Yves Cousteau has written that "the Aqualung is primitive and unworthy of contemporary levels of science." Lieutenant Commander Huout and Pierre Willm have described the *F.N.R.S.-3* bathyscaphe as a "proto-type, a blind, clumsy, limping monster." We are only at the frontier of the underwater world. As this book is being written scientists are designing new and better kinds of equipment with which to continue their explorations. The last chapter in man's conquest of the deep will be an exciting one and as challenging as the conquest of the moon and the planets.

4

Perils of the Deep

THE naked skin diver has only to worry about running out of breath or running into some dangerous sea creature. Although he may be bothered with bleeding from the nose, ears, and eyes after a particularly deep dive he is not subject to the mysterious illnesses that attack helmet divers and sandhogs working in diving bells. The disease most common to divers is characterized by pains in the joints or abdomen, so severe that the victim doubles up in agony. For this reason it is commonly called the bends. Unfortunately, pain is not the only symptom. Many times the victim is hopelessly paralyzed; other times he meets instant death. Many men were killed and maimed before a French physiologist named Paul Bert discovered the reason for the dreadful attacks. Oddly enough, he made his important discovery while studying the problems of balloonists and mountain climbers.

Bert knew that balloonists suffered attacks of the bends when they ascended to the thin air of great heights. He was therefore intrigued to learn that divers ascending to the surface from depths of over thirty feet often suffered the same symptoms. He looked for a common cause, and found it. In each case the individual had passed rapidly from an area of higher pressure to one of lower pressure.

The results of Bert's many detailed experiments were published in 1878 in a volume entitled *Barometric Pressure*. In it he explained that living beings react both physically and physiologically to changes in pressure. The studies made by Paul Bert revealed a close relationship between the problems of man's conquest of space and his conquest of the underwater depths. Today Bert is called the "father of aviation medicine," although he did not live to see an airplane.

Anyone who has dived to the bottom of a swimming pool is aware of the pressure of water. At a depth of eight to ten feet we feel this pressure as a pain in our ears. Most of us, however, tend to think of air as weightless. It is hard to believe that it exerts any pressure on our bodies. The truth is that we live at the bottom of a vast ocean of air. At sea level our bodies must withstand a pressure of 14.7 pounds on every square inch. This means that an average adult is under a total pressure of about fourteen tons. We do not feel the pressure because it is distributed evenly throughout our bodies and because we are perfectly adjusted to it. The moment we leave our particular pressure zone, however, we feel a change in pressure in our ears. Just as we feel an *increase* in pressure when we dive to the bottom of a swimming pool we feel a *decrease* in pressure when we drive to the top of a mountain or ascend in an airplane. This is because the pressure on the outside of the ear is different from the pressure on the inside. It can be equalized by permitting air to enter the inner ear through the Eustachian tubes. We do this by swallowing or blowing through the nose.

In water pressure increases at a rate of a little more than one pound for every two feet of descent. At a depth of thirty-three feet the pressure is exactly twice what it is at sea level. Since the solid parts of our bodies cannot be compressed it is in the air spaces—the lungs, sinus cavities, and ears—that we feel the pressure. The skin diver who goes to depths of thirty feet and more must become accustomed to having his lungs and ears subjected to severe strain. A diver breathing compressed air, however, whether he wears a helmet suit, Aqualung, or works bone dry in a diving bell, does not feel uncomfortable. The compressed air in his lungs, ears, and sinuses has a pressure exactly equal to that of the water around him. On the other hand, if this diver fills his lungs with compressed air at the bottom of a dive and then rises to the surface without exhaling the release of pressure will cause the air to expand and explode his lungs. It is absolutely necessary for a diver breathing compressed air to exhale as he ascends.

These are the purely physical aspects of pressure. If a diver stays more than a few minutes at a pressure considerably different from that to which his body is accustomed there is also a change in the composition of his blood. Blood, like most liquids, can dissolve gases like oxygen, carbon dioxide, and nitrogen. The amount of gas that will dissolve in a liquid depends on the pressure. The greater the pressure, the more gas that goes into solution. When the pressure is released, the gas comes out of solution, causing the liquid to fizz like soda pop.

Air is a combination of several gases. The two most important are oxygen—which makes up one-fifth of the air—and nitrogen—which makes up most of the remaining four-fifths. All animals, including man, must breathe oxygen to live. The nitrogen ordinarily passes in and out of the lungs unchanged. Nevertheless, it is extremely important that the oxygen be diluted in the proportion that nature intended. We can breathe pure oxygen only for short periods. As a steady diet it is poisonous.

A diver breathes an increased amount of air during the time he is under pressure. Although the oxygen in the air is almost completely used up by the body tissues greater amounts of nitrogen and carbon dioxide dissolve in the blood because of the increased pressure. If the diver ascends quickly and the pressure on his body is lowered suddenly the excess nitrogen in the blood stream comes out of solution and forms bubbles, which interfere with the circulation of the blood. In addition, the increased acidity of the blood, due to dissolved carbon dioxide, may also cause tiny blood clots to form. If either a blood clot or nitrogen bubble reaches one of the tiny blood vessels around the joints it restricts the flow of blood, causing severe pain. A common symptom known as sandhog's itch results when the circulation is cut off in the small blood vessels just beneath the skin. If there is a restriction of blood entering the brain the result may be paralysis. A bubble or clot reaching the heart or lungs results in asphyxia, choking, or instant death.

Since the symptoms occur as the result of decompression the disease is known medically as decompression sickness. It can be avoided by a very slow rate of ascent. If the diver returns gradually to atmospheric pressure the dissolved nitrogen and carbon dioxide can escape through the lungs and no dangerous clots or bubbles are formed. The first decompression tables were worked out for the British Admiralty in 1908. They gave the exact amount of time a diver had to remain underwater to decompress according to the depth and length of time of submersion. The main drawback to the use of these decompression tables was their serious time penalty. After a 250-foot dive of twenty minutes duration the decompression time was two hours and twenty-six minutes—more than seven times as long as the time spent on the bottom!

In 1935 three American physiologists—J.A. Hawkins, C.W. Schilling, and R.A. Hansen—made some important revisions in the decompression tables. Studies had shown that the concentration of nitrogen in the blood builds up rather slowly under pressure. They reasoned that if the periods of submersion were comparatively short (seventeen minutes total time for 150 feet, shorter periods for greater depths) the decompression time could be cut to a few minutes. Their revisions have since been incorporated into the United States Navy Standard Decompression Table.

In spite of all these precautions symptoms of decompression sickness occasionally occur among divers who descend frequently to appreciable depths. When they do, the diver must recompress, by returning as rapidly as possible to the pressure he has just left. Recompression forces the nitrogen bubbles back into solution in the blood stream. A much longer decompression time permits the nitrogen to come out of solution gradually and be expelled through the lungs.

The best way for a diver to recompress is in a recompression chamber. In the heavy steel-walled tank he can lie warm and relaxed, while he waits out the many hours necessary to assure safe decompression. In an emergency, however, he can always take a spare tank of compressed air and dive back down to the depth from which he ascended. The obvious drawback to this method is the long time during which the diver must hang suspended in the cold, dark water.

It is interesting that each man's tolerance to decompression sickness is somewhat different, depending on his weight and body build. The Greek sponge divers rarely take time to decompress. Instead, each diver learns through experience to esti-

DIVER EXPERIENCING NITROGEN NARCOSIS

mate rather accurately the length of time he can stay under water at a particular depth and yet ascend rapidly without ill effects. Decompression sickness strikes them down only when they misjudge their endurance. Inexperienced divers, finding themselves in unusual circumstances, are sometimes unable to estimate correctly the intimate relationship of depth to time. Older divers often become overconfident.

Nitrogen under pressure causes another strange disease, which has been called nitrogen narcosis or "rapture of the deep." At depths of two hundred feet or more a diver feels giddy and loses all sense of fear. He may even tear out his mouthpiece in the wild belief that like a fish he can breathe water. Or he may swim deeper and deeper, sublimely unaware that he is diving to his death. Several brave divers succumbed to this disease and lost their lives while trying to make depth records. Although nitrogen narcosis affects some people less than others, the practical limits of compressed-air diving are set firmly at two hundred feet.

In the United States experiments with artificial air have been made. The gas helium is substituted for nitrogen. Helium is odorless, tasteless, and easier to breathe than nitrogen. It is also only about half as soluble, and comes out of solution in the blood stream twice as fast. In an experimental dive in 1937 conducted by D. Edgar End and the late Max Gene Nohl of Milwaukee, Wisconsin, the diver was able to decompress in one-twenty-third of the usual time. Experiments have also shown that theoretically he can descend to a depth of a thousand feet before suffering intoxicating mental effects. However, the greatest depth reached by a diver breathing helium and oxygen is 600 feet.

An interesting experiment was made in 1945 by a Swedish diver named Arne Zetterstrøm. He devised a method of breathing a mixture of hydrogen and oxygen after it was discovered that this extremely explosive mixture becomes inert under great pressure. His experiment was successful and he reached a depth of 528 feet. Unfortunately he died before reaching the surface. Because of an unfortunate mistake he was hauled up too rapidly and died from explosive decompression. The experiment has never been repeated.

Scientists in several different countries are grappling with the problem of man's free descent into the depths. Perhaps it is possible to hope that someday a device will be invented that will permit him to breathe oxygen directly from the water as a fish does.

5

Operation Sea-Dig

ARE you ready to take part in an underwater excavation? Then come along and see what happens! The ship tugs gently at her anchor. Only a slight onshore breeze ruffles the surface of the billows. The sun is warm enough to make the water look inviting. It is a perfect day for a sea-dig.

In the prow of the ship four divers prepare to go below. They spread out their foam neoprene exposure suits, powder the slick inner surfaces, and with a wriggling, tugging kind of dance ease themselves into the skin-tight garments. Minutes later they are gasping with the heat. The black airtight suits look oppressive in the bright sunlight of the deck, but in the water they will be indispensable. These men are not going to splash about in the summer-warmed surface water. Their destination is to be the sea floor a hundred feet down. To get there they will pass through the thermocline, where the warmth of the surface changes abruptly to the chill of the depths.

One of the divers checks the tanks of compressed air with a pressure gauge to be sure they are full. The others ready their equipment: masks, fins, weight belts, knives, depth indicators, and watches. They screw the regulators, with their rubber mouthpiece and air-hoses, into place on the air tanks. Then, as last minute instructions are given them by the archaeologist, they help each other to put on the heavy tanks. Before putting on the masks they dip them into water and rub them with saliva. This simple but effective formula is used by divers everywhere to keep the glass face plates from fogging when contact is made with cold water. The accessories are buckled on and the divers walk to the railing of the ship. Seated on the gunwale they slip their swim fins on their feet, and at a signal from the lead diver they hold their masks tightly in place and fall over backward into the water. The sea feels delightfully cool to their overheated bodies. Surfacing, they swim to the yellow buoy that marks the descent line. This is a cord that has been dropped, with an anchor to mark the location of the underwater archaeological site.

At the descent line they signal each other to indicate all is well, and then with powerful strokes of their flippered feet they head for the bottom. On the way down the light about them fades into semidarkness and the pressure mounts in their ears. They swallow, blow through their noses, and the feeling of pressure is relieved. At the bottom they see each other as dark, shadowy figures. Once again they give the all-is-well signal and split up to work in pairs.

The first job is to photograph and measure the site, which in this case is an ancient wrecked ship. One of the divers is a trained photographer. He carries with him specially designed underwater still and motion picture cameras. While he makes a pictorial record of the site two other divers swim along the outlines of the wreck. One takes measurements with a steel tape measure, while the other records the figures on a slate, using a special underwater pencil. The fourth diver uses a similar slate to make a sketch of the site, on which he indicates the exact position of all exposed relics. These key procedures are repeated at each stage of the excavation. Only in this way can hundreds of details be recalled later by the archaeologist.

Next they pick up the ends of a large grid that has been lowered from the ship, and swimming slowly and carefully stretch it out over the site. The grid, which consists of a prefabricated network of light cable, is used to mark areas to be excavated. It also is a way of indicating the exact position of all finds. While the divers are working below their companions on board ship keep a constant and anxious eye on the exhaust bubbles. So long as the bubbles rise regularly to the surface they know that all is well. If something goes wrong, however, they are prepared to dive immediately to the rescue.

Down below the men check their watches. It has been twenty minutes since they left the ship. According to the United States Navy decompression tables they have five more minutes in which to make the gradual ascent to the surface.

They surface and swim to the side of the ship, where they are helped to climb up the rope ladder. The archaeologist eagerly takes their slates and studies them, while the divers strip off their equipment and rubber suits. Then the entire work crew goes into a huddle. The archaeologist plies them with one question after another.

"Were you able to tell which end was the prow of the ship?"

"Where is the greatest accumulation of material?"

"How deep do you think we will have to dig to reach the deck planking?"

They answer the questions carefully and to the best of their ability. Later the archaeologist will dive down to examine the wreck personally, but he like the other divers can spend only a limited time each day at the hundred-foot depth. He must depend to a great extent on information given him by his crew. After some minutes of consideration he decides on the next steps to be taken. Then he gives instructions to the alternate diving crew while they dress to make their dive.

When they are in the water a large rubber suction pipe is lowered to them and they swim with it to the bottom. The powerful suction in the pipe makes it writhe and twist like a giant snake. With it the divers "vacuum" litter and silt from specified areas in the grid. The mud and other debris that is sucked to the surface gushes into a sieve on board the ship, where a crew member on duty watches for small objects. The suction in this pipe is so powerful that it loosens and removes

the cementlike mixture of calcareous alga that often forms around objects buried in the sea. In areas where the mud and sand is loose and there is a current a high-powered water hose may be used to clear the site.

As the divers recover material from different parts of the grid they deposit it in separate wire baskets, which they have brought with them. The baskets when full are hoisted to the surface by a winch on the afterdeck of the ship.

The material is then cleaned of sea life and, if necessary, treated with a preservative. Other members of the crew mark and catalog each piece. Eventually all of the material will be turned over to the country in whose waters the ship was wrecked, but first it is studied by the archaeologist. He compares the material found under the sea with similar artifacts found in land excavations. In this way he determines the approximate age of the wreck and its origin. If material characteristic of one area is found stacked above material known to have come from another area the ship was obviously carrying cargo from several ports of call. It is not difficult in this case for the archaeologist to reconstruct the ship's itinerary. He studies the details of construction and any navigational instruments from the wreck, and draws conclusions about the technology of the period. Then, if enough information is present, he continues his study in libraries and archives. Eventually the jigsaw-puzzle pieces of evidence form a picture of human life in a bygone era. This is the ultimate goal of the underwater archaeologist.

There is an important difference between underwater archaeology and archaeological salvage. While the first seeks to recover objects from the deep to learn from them about the life and times of their makers, the second seeks only to recover them for their commercial or artistic value. Most of what has been called underwater archaeology in the past has been underwater salvage. Underwater archaeology as a science is only a little more than ten years old.

Nor are ancient shipwrecks the only underwater archaeological sites. In recent years archaeological discoveries have been made in oceans, seas, lakes, rivers, and even wells. They have ranged all the way from sunken ships to drowned villages and ceremonial offerings. However, in spite of the fact that similar tools and techniques are used to excavate all underwater sites sea-digging is not in itself a science. One must bear in mind that every archaeological item found below the waves was made by men who lived on dry land. Eventually the underwater archaeologist must compare his findings with those made by him or other archaeologists and historians on land. For this reason it is a new, fascinating, and highly specialized branch of archaeology.

There are four main types of underwater archaeological sites. The most common and least romantic are refuse sites. Anyone who has ever lived on a shore knows how typical it is for men to throw their trash into any convenient stream, lake, or sea. Fortunately, articles preserved underwater are often in far better condition than they would have been if discarded on land.

Submerged human habitations, such as campsites, villages, and even cities are a second kind of underwater archaeological site. The inundation of the site may be the result of an earthquake or a flood. It may have come about gradually due to a rise in the water level or a slow subsidence of the shoreline. Or it may have happened as dams and irrigation projects channeled rivers into new courses and flooded the land.

A third type of underwater archaeological site is a sacred body of water into which men have cast their religious offerings. These are called underwater shrines or places of offering and burial.

The fourth and best known underwater archaeological sites are shipwrecks. Before excavating them the archaeologist must learn all he can about the history and techniques of shipbuilding, ancient maritime commerce and laws, and navigation.

Underwater archaeology makes use of several new techniques. By all rights the archaeologist should learn to dive. Only in this way can he give proper direction to the excavation and the best interpretation to the evidence. Since the archaeologist acquires his knowledge through many years of training and experience it is far easier and more logical to teach diving to archaeologists than archaeology to divers.

Unfortunately almost none of the underwater archaeological sites investigated in past years have been supervised by diving archaeologists. Until the invention of the Cousteau-Gagnan Aqualung deep-sea diving was both difficult and dangerous. Also very few underwater sites were known in the early years of this century so that there was little reason for an archaeologist to learn to dive. In the past ten years Scuba diving has become a technique available to anyone. Many new underwater sites have been discovered and some of the most promising have been excavated. However, Scuba diving is best learned in youth. Most of the archaeologists who supervised these excavations were older men. They did not participate in the actual diving, but of necessity had to rely on second-hand observations given them by a crew of trained divers. Today a large number of young archaeologists are adding diving to the many other skills required in their profession.

How does one discover an underwater archaeological site? Occasionally it is obvious, just as crumbling ruins are obvious signs of an archaeological site on dry land. Far more often it takes an alert and trained eye.

Mention a sunken ship to someone and ask him to describe it. The chances are he will imagine the vessel to be intact, except for perhaps a gaping hole. He may expect the rigging to be broken and draped with seaweed. If he is particularly imaginative he may even visualize a skeleton, the remains of the gallant captain who went down with his ship. He may also think happily of a treasure chest, the lid open and golden Spanish coins spilling out over the sand. In his imagination fish swim in and out through the portholes, and deep within the hold of the ship, invisible except for two lidless eyes, hides a giant octopus.

Does the picture sound familiar? It should. It has been the subject of countless Sunday supplement adventure stories, movies, books, and television scenarios. But if, as a diver, you start out looking for just such a wreck, even discounting the octopus and the treasure chest, you are bound to be disappointed. In spite of all that has been written to the contrary such a wreck usually doesn't and couldn't exist.

If the ship went down in fairly shallow water close to shore it was battered beyond recognition in a matter of weeks by the action of the surf. Even if it sank into quiet, deeper water the wood and any other organic material was attacked by bacteria, shipworms, starfish, and other destructive crustaceans. After a hundred years most of the wooden parts of a wrecked ship are completely eaten away.

But the sea, like the land, can also preserve. There are many areas of the ocean where coral grows so abundantly that any foreign object left on the sea floor is soon covered with a thick coral encrustation. This deposit protects the object from further damage.

An even better preservative is mud. If the ship sank in a section where the sea bed was soft the weight of the vessel carried it well down into the bed of ooze. If the wreck was near the mouth of a river it was completely covered with silt in a matter of years, sometimes even months. Such a quick burial would preserve most of the wood and metal. An ancient ship preserved in this way is an archaeological treasure. However, because it is so well hidden it is not likely to be discovered by a diver, but rather in the course of dredging operations. Another preservative is made up of the bodies of millions of tiny sea animals called diatoms. It forms slowly through the ages, and if a ship lies for a long enough time on the sea floor, say a thousand years, its remains are eventually covered with this fossil mud.

Before this happens most wooden parts are consumed by sea animals. The ship's grave is a mound of earth, marked with protruding bits of metal or pottery or stones from her ballast.

Although many of the most important underwater archaeological sites have been discovered by accident some have been deliberately sought out. Between 1935 and 1937 the remains of the Phoenician ports of Tyre and Sidon were excavated, mapped, and photographed by the French Jesuit scholar Father A. Poidebard. He knew where to begin his search from a study of old documents and from aerial photographs, which indicated the shadowy outlines of submerged wharves and pilings. An American by the name of Edward Thompson began his historic excavation of an ancient Mayan well in Yucatan, Mexico, after studying early documents of the Spanish conquest. He read that sacrificial offerings and even human victims had been thrown into the well in honor of the rain god. His wild hunch to investigate the well paid off, and he recovered quite a treasure. Several historic ships of the British colonial period in America have been tracked down through a study of early naval documents.

Even though the archaeologist has located an underwater site, whether accidentally or through an examination of historical or archaeological evidence, he is still not ready to begin excavating . Not every underwater site can be excavated. The depth is of great importance. Since divers breathing compressed air cannot work at depths greater than two hundred feet anything deeper than that is, for all practical purposes, inaccessible. Below a hundred and twenty feet the water is very cold, even in tropical or subtropical regions. The time that a diver can spend on the bottom is short, and much valuable time is wasted in descending and ascending.

If the site is easily accessible from the shore the excavation headquarters can be located nearby on the land. If not, the archaeologists and their crew of divers must work off a ship. At present only a few underwater research ships are in existence.

Of them, the beautiful *Calypso*, belonging to Captain Cousteau, is the most outstanding. It has been fitted with many special features designed to aid an underwater research program. A large winch on the afterdeck is used to haul heavy objects from the water. There is a special underwater exit so that the divers do not have to risk being battered against the ship by a rough surf. On the prow, below the water level, is an observation chamber. A diver lying in this can keep track of what lies below, and still remain snug and dry. The *Calypso* sonar equipment is sensitive enough to draw a picture of the ocean floor and indicate even so small an object as a pottery jar.

Sonar, sometimes called echo sound, is one of the most useful devices for locating shipwrecks. The name comes from the words sound navigation and ranging. The depth of the water is measured automatically and continuously as the ship plows ahead at full speed. Sound waves are directed toward the ocean floor and the rebounding echoes are picked up on a receiver which electronically translates the intervening time into

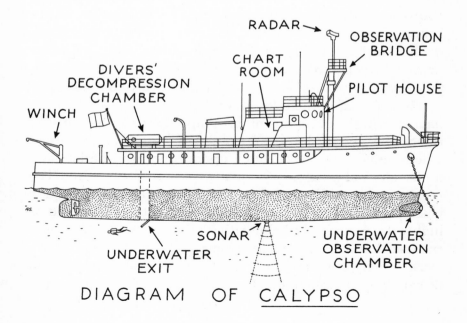

DIAGRAM OF CALYPSO

depths. The sound waves also activate a pencil, which draws a graph of the sea bottom. This is called a bathygram, and any sunken object over which the ship passes is indicated on it.

The *Calypso* is equipped with electronic underwater metal detectors, which can "see" through murky water, mud, and even thick encrustations of coral. It also carries underwater motorized units, such as electric scooters and propeller-driven "wings," to transport the divers on their underwater explorations. With these units the divers can travel further, faster, and with less effort. One of the latest is Cousteau's "Diving Saucer," a two-man submarine which can go as deep as 1,500 feet. A remote-control system that will send an unmanned ship with a television camera to scout along the sea bottom is under development. A small Italian warship, the *Daino,* has been fitted for underwater investigation by Italian archaeologists. Professor Nino Lamboglia directs the research activities and the crew of divers from the experimental center for underwater archaeology at Leghorn, Italy. The *Sea Diver,* owned by Ed Link and used by the Smithsonian Institution Marine Archaeology Project, is still smaller, but is equipped for work in the Caribbean.

Ships such as the *Calypso,* the *Daino,* and the *Sea Diver* are expensive to own and operate. Most archaeologists must be content with far less luxurious and convenient surroundings.

The basic equipment for an underwater excavation, as we have seen at the beginning of this chapter, consists primarily of the Scuba diver's dress and gear. Although there are times when helmet divers are called upon to perform underwater archaeological tasks the job usually goes to a Scuba diver. The reason is simple. The Scuba diver can work on soft, muddy bottoms, in swift currents, or in a tangle of debris that would be highly dangerous for a helmet diver. Even more to the point is the fact that he can swim into inaccessible locations and can work directly from shore. His equipment is easily portable and he can dress himself unaided.

Before beginning an excavation a permit must be obtained from the local government. According to international law every wreck has a legal owner, and the legal owner of an ancient ship is the country in whose waters it was wrecked. This law has been expanded to apply to any underwater archaeological site. Unless arrangements have been made in advance all excavated material must be turned over to a local museum. Of course, if a diver finds a few cannon balls or an amphora he can recover them without getting special permission. He may keep them so long as he does not take them out of the country.

These laws may seem burdensome and in some cases unnecessary, but they serve a very worth-while purpose. In the last century and the early years of the present century many archaeological sites on land were looted by treasure hunters. As a result much priceless information was irreplaceably lost. The same thing is happening today to underwater archaeological sites. Amphora hunting has become a hobby in the Mediterranean. It has become such a craze that some professional divers have made a business of ransacking archaeological sites to find amphoras to sell to tourists, who are unable to find their own.

Although many divers like to call themselves amateur archaeologists they do not have the training, experience, and knowledge to excavate a site by themselves. Often their idea of excavation is to haul off as much material as possible, without regard for the many details which are so important and meaningful to the scientist. They may overlook or discard items that are broken and ugly, not realizing the important clues that they may provide. Whenever a diver discovers an underwater archaeological site he should report it, no matter how unimportant it may seem to him. His finds may be more significant than he realizes.

6

Twenty Centuries under the Sea

O N THE Greek islands in the blue Aegean Sea live a hardy breed of men. Their profession is an old and honorable one. It has been passed down for countless generations from father to son. These men are the *sphoungarades,* Greek sponge divers, whose skill and daring have made them the heroes of the fisherfolk. Their adventures are told and retold, and not infrequently greatly exaggerated, wherever men of the sea congregate. Since the beginning of the twentieth century most have worked in helmet diving suits. Nevertheless they can skin dive to depths of a hundred feet or more. But like most heroes many die a hero's death. They are very much aware of the fatal consequences of too frequent or prolonged diving. Perhaps it is because many of them die young that they work and play so recklessly.

The sponge-diving season is brief and there is stiff competition. During the short campaign they waste not one minute, but work continuously until even the strongest are exhausted. As many sponges as possible are gathered and loaded on the ship. When the catch is sold the sponge fishermen jubilantly set sail for home, rich men according to their simple standards. On their return they celebrate joyously and riotously their annual triumph over the sea.

Of all the *sphoungarades* the most renowned come from the island of Symē in the Dodecanese islands of southeastern

Greece. It is appropriate that these sturdy men should have been the first heroes of underwater archaeology.

In the year 1900 a crew of sponge divers were on their way home from North Africa, where the finest sponges grow on the sea floor. Their slim caïques were equipped with sails, but in addition each carried twenty-two oars for use in calm weather. Almost within sight of the Greek mainland, but still a long way from their native island, the ships were caught in a howling gale and driven off course. Unable to continue they took shelter off the barren, almost uninhabited islet of Antikýthēra, and anchored some twenty-five yards from the headland which borders the little harbor.

The men were restless and impatient with the delay. At last the captain suggested that they wait out the wind by looking for sponges. Diver Elias Stadiatis was helped into his helmet suit and slipped over the side. When he reached the bottom, 150 feet down, he was struck with amazement. Before him in the extraordinarily clear water were huge figures of men, women, and horses strewn about on the sea floor and partially buried in sand and mud. Some were the white of marble; others dark bronze. Knowing that no one on board ship would believe him without evidence he pulled at a dark protruding hand. A whole bronze arm came out of the sand. Stadiatis signaled by four tugs on his line that he wanted to ascend, and was hauled back to the surface.

As soon as Captain Demetrios Kondos, himself a master diver, had seen the arm and heard of the surprising discovery he called for his dresser and was helped into his diving suit. Clutching a tape measure he went below to take careful measurements.

Within minutes of their arrival on Symē the entire island was electrified with the news. That night Captain Kondos called a meeting of island elders to decide on the proper course of action. Everyone could guess at the value of the material and

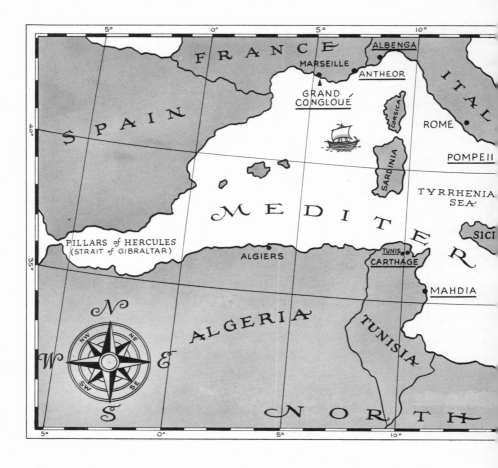

the money it would bring from art dealers. They also realized
that it would take heavy lifting equipment to raise most of the
statues from the sea bed. After considerable debate it was decided that Kondos and Stadiatis should take the bronze arm to
Athens and report the discovery to the Greek government.

The two sponge divers, skilled as they were with life on the
sea, must have looked bewildered and out-of-place in the busy
capital city. Fortunately the bronze arm they carried was
ample proof of the authenticity and value of their discovery.
The archaeologists in Athens were most impressed. In fact they

could hardly get to work fast enough. Kondos agreed that he and his men would work with them to recover the treasures, with a bonus to be paid for each piece brought up from the bottom. It was further arranged that a ship from the Greek navy would assist them in lifting the huge pieces measured by Captain Kondos.

Not only was this the first underwater archaeological excavation, it was also the first one to be carried out entirely by Greek archaeologists. For two thousand years men from other countries had been carrying off masterpieces of Greek sculpture, but at the end of the nineteenth century a law was finally enacted forbidding the transport of Greek antiquities beyond the national borders. The local archaeologists were eager to rediscover what still remained of their national heritage.

Unfortunately the Antikýthēra project was ill-fated from the very beginning. After spending the entire summer of 1900 in preparation, the operation was finally begun in late November. The divers had been at work only three hours the first day when a storm came up which forced the ships to take shelter. During the first dive, however, they recovered a life-size bronze head, two large marble statues, and several smaller pieces. The weather continued bad, and each new attempt was interrupted after only a few hours. The six divers worked to the limit of their endurance. With their primitive equipment they could stay only five minutes on the sea floor. The 150- to 170-foot depth was beyond their usual working range.

Although the first sculptures had come up easily later ones had to be dug out of the sand and mud. Stiff, wet ropes were tied around the slimy bodies of marble and bronze and securely knotted so that the crane could pull them to the surface. Sometimes the rope slipped and a day's efforts were lost as the statue sank back into the ooze, crushing other pieces beneath it. On the very best days a total of one hour of work at the bottom was all that was possible.

Nine weary months passed, during all of which the ships were in constant danger of being dashed against the rocky cliff. In the spring four new divers were brought to replace the exhausted but valiant original group. Two had been permanently disabled and one man had died from the bends.

It was a heroic task but the results today fill a long gallery in the National Museum in Athens. The finest of the big bronze statues is the fourth century "Athlete," a noble young god or hero slightly larger than life size. He is none the worse for his long rest under the sea. The marble statues did not fare so well. The parts that were buried in the sand or mud are still in good condition, but the areas exposed to the sea water are horribly corroded and eaten away by shellfish. They look like the victims of some terrible disease. In some cases all that is left of an arm or leg is a spindly stump; what was a noble head is a formless lump.

One extraordinary find enabled archaeologists to date the wreck to the first century before Christ, and gave them new knowledge of ancient Greek scientific technology. The object, a Greek computer, was a clocklike mechanism used to calculate the motions of the stars and planets. It could easily have been overlooked during the underwater search as a few insignificant pieces of corroded metal. Eight months after the end of the Antikýthēra excavation Valerios Stäis, an archaeologist at the Greek National Museum, recognized the fragments as pieces of a mechanism. They first caught his eye because of their inscriptions. The epigrapher, Benjamin Dean Meritt, later identified the forms of the letters as those of the first century B.C.

The fragments were examined by every available archaeologist. Most agreed it was some sort of astronomical device, but the thick covering of calcified material and the corrosion concealed so much detail that no one could be sure just how it had been used. Fifty-five years passed before an archaeologist by the name of Derek de Solla Price began the delicate work of joining the pieces together. The results of his work were both spectacular and surprising.

The computer consisted of a box with dials on the outside and a very complex assembly of gear wheels within. It resembled an astronomical clock, similar in concept to those of medieval Europe. In fact, according to the archaeologist, the Greek computer must have been the ancestor of all clockwork. Similar astronomical computers were described by Arab astronomers as early as 1000 A.D. Apparently they learned about them from Greek writings and passed the idea along to Europe about the time of the Crusades.

Until the discovery of the Antikýthēra computer no one

would have believed that the ancient Greeks had reached such an advanced level of scientific technology. Only the accidental underwater preservation of fragments that would have crumbled to dust had they been buried in the earth brought this knowledge to light.

Although the material recovered from the wreck was definitely of Grecian origin, Greece in the first century B.C. had neither a naval or a merchant fleet. The archaeologists concluded that the vessel was Roman. Why was a Roman ship carrying this load of Greek bronze and marble statuary? To answer this question we will have to look in on Greece and Rome about the middle of the first century B.C.

Three hundred years earlier the Greek city-states had been conquered by a powerful neighbor to the north, Macedonia. Even though Greece had flourished under the brief but momentous reign of Alexander the Great the Greek leaders had objected to his dictatorial methods. After Alexander's death there was a scuffle for the succession, and many of the Greek cities took this opportunity to try again to liberate themselves. They might have succeeded if they hadn't been plagued by an age-old Greek problem. They couldn't work together as a nation. Their efforts were weakened by a struggle for leadership among the Greeks themselves. In the meantime, on the other side of the Ionian Sea, another city was struggling for power. This was Rome in the days before she created the greatest empire of the ancient world. Rome was having some vexing problems of her own with her powerful competitor, Carthage, which was situated on the African shore of the Mediterranean Sea. In a series of conflicts called the Punic Wars Rome fought Carthage and finally was victorious. Then, angered with Philip V of Macedonia for having formed an alliance with Carthage, Rome also decided to conquer Macedonia. The Greek city-states gave Rome active support in the two Macedonian Wars. However, even though Rome was again the victor the

Greek cities gained nothing for their alliance. They were declared independent, but Roman leaders dictated policy and eventually some of the cities were even made to pay tribute to Rome. The Greeks discovered that they had exchanged a lenient master for a much more severe one. When Corinth showed signs of restlessness and possible revolt it was completely destroyed. The Roman general Lucius Cornelius Sulla ordered a massacre of Athens in 86 B.C. By the time of the Antikýthēra wreck Greece had endured more than a hundred years of Roman domination. All signs of Greek resistance had died out, the Greek economy had collapsed, and still the devastation continued. Beginning in 48 B.C. three Roman civil wars were fought on Greek soil. At the same time that the Romans were crushing the last sparks of Greek power and prosperity they were eagerly helping themselves to Greek culture, which they greatly admired. Whole ships were loaded with confiscated Greek statuary, and hundreds of Greek artists and scholars were ordered to Rome.

With this historical background we can look again at the treasure salvaged from the Antikýthēra wreck. The fact that the bronze statues were taken from some Greek temple is obvious. The leaden bases were ripped and bent, showing how they had been torn from their stone pedestals. All of the bronze statues were valuable, but one of them, the "Athlete," was made in the style of the fourth century B.C. It was already four hundred years old when it was stolen, and must have been a priceless antique. The quality of workmanship of the marble statues was inferior. The archaeologists readily identified them as commercial copies of famous originals. They had no great value and were hardly worth confiscating. Whoever took them was either in a great hurry, or else was no judge of art. The looters, of course, were Romans, and the ship was on its way back to Italy when it ran into a storm, probably not unlike the one that drove Captain Kondos and his sponge divers to

Antikýthēra. The Roman ship was not so lucky, and it sank. It is poetic justice that the treasure was recovered at last by Greeks, and returned to the place of its origin.

Only a portion of the material from the Antikýthēra wreck was ever recovered from the sea. Although the discoveries had caused tremendous interest among archaeologists and artists the project was abandoned. It was a sad fact that the Greek navy simply did not have the facilities to carry it further. An Italian salvage company offered to do the work, but demanded in payment one-half of all the salvaged treasure. Since by Greek law it is forbidden to give works of art as compensation the project was closed and gradually the excitement died down.

7

"Nothing Since Pompeii . . . !"

THE Antikýthēra wreck had barely been forgotten when the Greek sponge divers did it again. Just seven years after the first underwater archaeological discovery another of even greater importance was made three miles off the coast of North Africa, near the town of Mahdia in Tunisia. Some sponge divers, working their favorite hunting grounds, spotted a row of huge cylindrical objects half-buried in the mud at a depth of 127 feet. They investigated what they first thought were cannons, and found the wreckage of a Roman ship loaded with art treasures. This time the Greek divers did not report their discovery. Instead they quietly brought up pieces of statuary that were lying loose on the bottom and sold them in the local market.

It was not long, however, before this unexpected flood of new material came to the attention of Alfred Merlin, the French government Director of Antiquities in Tunisia. Noticing that many of the pieces were encrusted with marine life he suspected the Greek sponge fishermen and asked Admiral Jean Baehme, in command of the French Tunisian Naval District, to send navy divers to investigate their underwater activities. Admiral Baehme reported that what had looked like cannons were actually Greek Ionic columns, and that they marked, as the Greeks already knew, the wreck of a ship of classical antiquity.

Merlin quickly sent word of the discovery to the famous

French archaeologist and art historian Salomon Reinach. Reinach, in turn, was so impressed that he began immediately to raise money for a full-scale archaeological excavation. Excitedly he declared, "Nothing comparable has come to light since Pompeii and Herculaneum!"

An American by the name of James Hazen Hyde generously donated $25,000, a very large sum of money at the beginning of the twentieth century. The project was put in charge of a Lieutenant Tavera, in command of the French government tug *Cyclope*. Civilian divers were brought from Italy and Greece; at that time they were the men most experienced in working at a depth of twenty-one fathoms. They were outfitted with the latest in helmet diving suits. Nevertheless, in spite of the strong financial support of private citizens and of the French government, it took five years and four expeditions to clear the greater part of the vessel.

The weather was again a problem. Often a sudden storm came up during the night and carried away the buoys marking the limits of the search area. Then the whole laborious task of locating the wreck had to begin over again. The depth of 127 feet, although not as great as at Antikýthera, still made diving hazardous, and before the excavation was over several divers were incapacitated by the bends. Another complication was that the divers had to work almost blind in a sea of mud. They could not find words strong enough to express their disgust at the clouds of black ooze that swirled around them at every movement. It was this mud, however, that had preserved the marble sculptures from the ravages of salt water and shellfish.

One can imagine the excitement that greeted each new find. Far below the surface, lost in a world of liquid mud, men searched for history. The only one on board ship who could make a guess at what was happening below was the man on duty at the air pump. He kept tight hold of the safety line. When he received the signal that a diver wanted to come up he alerted the archaeologists. Crew members, scientists, and guests

peered anxiously over the side, as the diver was slowly hoisted to the surface. If in his arms he held some treasure, encrusted with shellfish and draped with seaweed, eager hands reached out to receive it. If, as often happened, he arrived exhausted and empty-handed, there was a sigh of disappointment. Then a fresh diver was dressed, and he descended to carry on the work.

A considerable treasure was taken from the wreck. Among the cargo were sixty Ionic marble columns and other architectural pieces, which apparently were building materials for a complete temple or villa. In addition to numerous commercial-quality marble statues, there were bronze lamps, candelabra, ornamental pieces of couches and chairs, and a few exceptionally fine bronze statues. One statue represented the winged Greek god of love, Eros, leaning on a pillar. At the top of the pillar was the bearded head of Dionysus, the Greek god of wine and merrymaking. The figure was signed by the well-known Greek sculptor Boëthus, who lived about the turn of the second century B.C.

Both Reinach and Merlin made a careful study of the Mahdia artifacts. They agreed that the ship must have sailed from Athens. The white, heavily-veined marble from which the columns were cut could only have come from nearby Mount Hymettus. The signed statue by Boëthus indicated that the tragedy could not have occurred before the end of the third century. Because of this date the Mahdia vessel, like the one wrecked off Antikýthēra, must have been Roman.

The archaeologists came to widely different conclusions concerning the presence of a Roman ship in North African waters. Salomon Reinach was convinced that the ship, like the Antikýthēra vessel, was loaded with booty from Greece. He even went so far as to tie it in with the massacre and looting of Athens by the Roman general Sulla in 86 B.C. The vessel, he decided, had been on its way to Rome when it was blown far off course across the Mediterranean. Alfred Merlin argued that although some of the Mahdia cargo was magnificent a great deal of it was of such commonplace commercial quality that even Sulla, with his notoriously bad taste, would not have bothered with it. Moreover, this was the period of Roman colonization in North Africa. It was more likely, he thought, that the cargo had been ordered by some Roman building contractor in Mahdia.

Upholding Merlin's theory is the fact that the ship was apparently heading toward Mahdia when it sank. All five of the ship's anchors, including the heavy sheet anchor used only in the most dire emergency, were recovered on the landward side of the vessel. This indicated that the anchors had been cast overboard in an effort to prevent the craft from being blown out to sea. The heavy load of marble must have shifted in such a way that the vessel began to ship water, and, completely swamped, went to the bottom within sight of land.

Unfortunately the money ran out and the excavation came to an end before these two learned men could prove their theories one way or the other. The material was taken to the Alaoui museum in Bardo, Tunis, where it was forgotten by all but a few specialists.

After the Antikythēra and Mahdia excavations very little was heard about underwater archaeology for almost thirty years. However, between 1935 and 1937 Father Poidebard carried on his little publicized excavations of the underwater remains of Tyre and Sidon. It was because Father Poidebard was searching for some underwater remains of the port of Carthage near the modern city of Tunis that the Mahdia wreck was rediscovered.

In 1948 the Jesuit scholar was with Captain Cousteau, Philippe Tailliez, Frédéric Dumas, and their crew aboard the French navy research ship, the *Élie Monnier*. The divers could find nothing at the supposed site of Carthage. However, while searching the Tunisian archives for documentary information Cousteau and Poidebard came across Lieutenant Tavera's report of the Mahdia excavation. This report, and a look at the material in the Bardo museum, so fired their imaginations that they decided to devote two weeks to a new investigation of the wreck.

Lieutenant Tavera had carefully recorded the position of the underwater site by lining it up with three points on shore: a ruin, an isolated tree, and a thicket. Unfortunately after thirty-five years these reference points were no longer visible. Cousteau and his crew had to use all their ingenuity to relocate the vessel.

They had only two facts with which to work. The exact distance from shore—three miles—was known and so was the exact depth at which the wreck had been found. The first step, therefore, was to use sonar equipment to locate an area that met these two conditions. The *Élie Monnier* began making large sweeps back and forth in the general area. Finally the search was narrowed to nine acres of sea bed. A huge grid, patterned like an American football field but covering an area of 100,000 square feet, was then laid out under water. Divers were sent down to swim along the strips and survey the sea floor yard by yard. After two days the grid had been examined thoroughly, but there was no sign of the wreck. A member of the crew Lieutenant Jean Alinat, put on his Aqualung and was towed by the *Élie Monnier* on an undersea sled around the outside of the grid. He found nothing. Three more days passed without results.

By this time the divers were exhausted, discouraged, and thoroughly mystified at their failure to find any sign of the ship. On the sixth day they were ready to give up the search when Commandant Philippe Tailliez, towed on a weighted line behind a small launch, finally spotted the huge columns and sent up a yellow signal buoy to mark the spot. Minutes later he popped to the surface, tore out his mouthpiece, and shouted the good news. As Tailliez wrote in his book, *To Hidden Depths:*

> The sight was a thrilling one. All that remained of the Mahdia galley after 2,000 years amounted to a collection of widely spaced lumps, with a number of columns arranged in four main rows. The general effect, in spite of the disturbance caused by the Greek divers, was overwhelmingly that of a ship, 36 feet wide by 120 feet long, lying on a north-south axis. Fragments of the ribs of the hull, of the deck, and of the keel were visible beneath the columns, or in the intervals between them.

So much time had been lost in locating the wreck that only a week remained for the investigation. The first job was to enlarge the breach made by the helmet divers in 1913. They did this by raising four columns, which were secured by slings and hoisted by derrick onto the afterdeck of the *Élie Monnier*. The derrick was hard put to lift them. The largest column weighed three tons. Next the divers moved in with a water hose to clear away the mud. Two feet below the level of the sea floor they uncovered the ship's solid top deck, sheathed with leaden plates. Seeing this, Cousteau concluded that the lower two-thirds of the ship was so well buried that it was probably still intact.

In striking contrast to their predecessors the Cousteau divers had no difficulties working at the 127-foot depth. They had the advantage of the latest diving tables, worked out by their own Lieutenant Alinat.

In order to make efficient use of the Alinat tables Cousteau organized a system of diving shifts according to a rigid time-table. When it was time for one group of divers to come up a rifle blast was fired into the water. The divers were under strict orders to drop whatever they were doing at the instant they heard the blast and ascend immediately. The penalty for even a few minutes' delay might be a crippling case of the bends.

Except for the columns very little was recovered from the Mahdia vessel during the second excavation. Cousteau decided to use his limited time to study the condition of the wreck rather than to acquire a great load of treasure. His observations convinced him that amidships there was still untouched cargo. He also reasoned that an excavation of the forecastle of the ship would bring to light many of the personal possessions belonging to the men who sailed it. In Greek and Roman times, as today, this section was used as living quarters for the crew. A small lamp with the charred wick still in position gave a better clue to the age of the vessel. Its characteristic shape showed that it was made at the very end of the second century B.C. Since it was in use the day the ship foundered, the event probably occurred early in the first century B.C.

Cousteau and his crew came up with one more theory worth considering. Many of the marble columns looked new. Others were unfinished. Can it be, they asked, that the Romans went in for "prefabricated" temples? Historical records tell us that wherever the Romans colonized, they built in the same elegant Greek architectural style. However, they could not always find the necessary building materials and artisans. It is quite possible that they ordered the structural elements for their temples and villas shipped from workshops in Greece and assembled them where they were needed.

Mahdia has still not revealed all its secrets. Who can tell what might be discovered if the main skeleton of the ship were to be cleared? Cousteau would like to have probed deeper, but as an officer in the French navy he had other commitments. Numerous archaeologists have been tempted by the proposition, but have lacked the money for a full-scale excavation. Professional divers demand and deserve high wages. Powerful lifting and dredging equipment is needed to carry out an underwater excavation. Water hoses or suction pumps are necessary to clear away the mud. The crew must work from some sort of boat. All this special equipment is very costly.

Any attempt to excavate the wreck without proper equipment and skilled personnel would be doomed to failure. What is more important it might destroy the evidence forever. We will have to wait for the next chapter of the Mahdia story. In the meantime we can at least be reassured that what has been preserved in mud for two thousand years will not deteriorate noticeably in the next twenty.

8

Grand Congloué

COUSTEAU and his crew of the *Élie Monnier* had only the brief-
est taste of underwater archaeology during the Mahdia
excavation. Four years later they bit into a chunk of truly impressive proportions. In the meantime Cousteau acquired his
own ship, the *Calypso,* and was detached by the French navy to
organize oceanographic research. One of his first projects was
the investigation of some shipwrecks off the coast of Marseille.

So it was that on an August day in 1952 Cousteau and the
French archaeologist Fernand Benoît stood together on the
deck of the *Calypso.* The sleek white ship steamed slowly through
the blue waters of the Mediterranean. On one side rose the
towering white limestone cliffs of the French mainland. On the
other were scattered islands so bleak, barren, and uninhabited
as to look ghostly in the bright sunlight. One of them, tiny
Grand Congloué, was their destination.

The project had begun with a chance bit of information
passed on to Frédéric Dumas by a disabled free-lance Aqualung diver. Some months earlier the diver had been brought
into the French navy's undersea research group at Toulon with
his legs paralyzed from an attack of the bends. His life was
saved through the quick use of a recompression chamber, but
the loss of circulation in his toes started a gangrenous infection
that necessitated their immediate amputation. The diver remained in the hospital six months, during which time Dumas
visited him weekly. Grateful to Dumas for his kindness, he di-

vulged a secret. On a ledge below the island of Grand Congloué he described a bed of large, delectable lobsters. It was
marked, he said, by a natural stone arch and a mound of old
pots. Dumas was fond of lobsters, to be sure, but he was more
interested in the reference to the old pots. He suspected that
they were Greek or Roman amphoras, marking the grave of
an ancient ship, and suggested to Cousteau that they make an
investigation.

The *Calypso* drew up close to the rocky shore of Grand Congloué and dropped anchor. Dumas, the first to go below,
quickly found the underwater arch in a blanket of live coral.
He swam west and passed the lobster bed, but found no sign of
the jars. When his time ran out he surfaced and Cousteau
dived down to continue the search. The explorer's trained eyes
darted back and forth, as he examined the weed- and sponge-
covered rocks for the graceful outline of an amphora. He swam
the 450 feet around the island, once dipping as low as 200 feet.
And then, unexpectedly, he found them. There, on a mud shelf
130 feet below the surface, were hundreds of amphoras tumbled about between stacks of bowls and dishes. Cousteau
grasped three stacked wine cups and a corroded bronze boat
hook and kicked for the surface. Professor Benoît, waiting at
the gunwale, saw Cousteau's hand come out of the water and
shouted, "They're Campanian!"

The French archaeologist had good reason to be excited. The
shape of the bowls indicated that they were the Campanian
ware typical of the third century B.C. The *Calypso* expedition
had stumbled on a cargo ship more than one hundred and fifty
years older than the Mahdia and Antikýthēra vessels.

To tell the story of the shipwreck of Grand Congloué we
have to go back 2,200 years to the Greek isle of Dēlos. Today
this sun-baked island in the Aegean Sea is almost deserted, but
it was once a sacred island dedicated to the Greek god Apollo.
It was then the scene of a great Greek settlement. Among its

residents was a newly-naturalized Greek citizen of Roman birth by the name of Marcus Sestius.

Sestius was a shipowner and wine exporter, and a wealthy and successful one at that. He had markets as far away as the Roman colony of Massilia, which is now the port of Marseille on the French coast. The Greeks and Romans who lived in this far-flung outpost of civilization paid excellent prices for sweet, spicy Aegean wine and pretty pottery dishes. There was a certain risk involved in sending a shipment such a great distance, even by sea, but the profits were large. Sestius was willing to gamble on his luck.

One day, perhaps it was in the year 240 B.C., Sestius went down to the wharves to oversee the loading of the Grand Congloué vessel. He looked with pride at his handsome ship. It was huge, over one hundred feet long, and capable of carrying a cargo of ten thousand amphoras. Since each wine-filled amphora weighed about a hundred pounds we can guess that the ship when fully loaded would have weighed at least a thousand tons. It was much too big and heavy to be manned by rowers. In all probability it carried a great single mast and square sail of sewn bull hides. Sestius felt satisfied that the ship was in good condition for the voyage. Certainly no cost had been spared in the construction. He thought proudly of the sturdy keel of solid oak and of the carefully seasoned and lacquered Aleppo pine and Lebanon cedar that had been brought from the Near East for the hull and ribbing.

To the bottom of the hold, under the heavy lead-plated main deck, went jar after jar of Greek wine. Then, only half-loaded, the ship sailed west through the Greek islands.

Ahead lay the most dangerous part of the voyage. It was the dreaded crossing of the Ionian Sea between Greece and Italy. With luck and a steady wind the sailors could expect to cross it in four days. However, if becalmed or caught by a storm the outcome could be disastrous. Poseidon, the Greek god of the sea, must have blessed their voyage by sending them

good weather. They reached the coast of Italy without incident.

The vessel steered its way through the Strait of Messina between the island of Sicily and the tip of Italy. It then followed the coast north to dock at a port near what is now the modern city of Naples. In the third century B.C. the many colonies established by the Greeks in southern Italy were busy and growing. Their special products were wine and polished black dinnerware, which they produced in mass quantities for export to other Greek colonies. It was a load of this black pottery that was now carried aboard the ship of Marcus Sestius and stowed above the Greek wine. Finally the main deck was covered with slender Italian amphoras. Piled three deep, each of the urns contained several gallons of red Latium wine.

When the ship once more set out to sea it was badly over-loaded and plowed heavily through the waves. In the evening the sailors sat by their cooking fires, built on a hearth on the poop deck, and watched the smoke drift over the wake. Per-haps they thought of home, far away in the Greek islands. Or perhaps, like sailors anywhere, they were looking forward to the joys of shore leave, once they reached Marseille. Certainly they were relieved that the long and dangerous voyage was nearly over. One night they may have decided to celebrate and drunk too freely of the tempting cargo of wine; possibly a sud-den storm was responsible for the tragedy. Whatever hap-pened, tragedy struck with a sickening thud; there was a grind-ing and crashing of ships' timbers. The vessel plowed into a pocket of rock on the eastern cape of Grand Congloué island and its stern quarters were ripped open. It sank quickly and landed keel down on a sloping shelf of rock. One of the anchors, thrown out as a last desperate attempt to avoid the catastrophe, caught on a ledge seventy-five feet above the ship.

As far as Marcus Sestius was concerned this was the end of his great vessel. We can wonder whether he ever recovered financially from the loss, but we will never know.

For almost 2,200 years the ship lay undisturbed in her grave at the bottom of the sea. The steep limestone walls and the 140-foot depth at which the ship had settled prevented it from being broken and scattered by the surf. Bacteria and shipworms feasted on the exposed timbers of the superstructure, but the heavy lead sheathing protected the hull and decks. The pressure of the sea popped the corks into the wine jars. For a brief moment the sea was stained red. Sponges, starfish, and sea urchins came to live in and upon the wreck, and fish darted among the jars and broken dishes. Generations of octopuses made their homes in the wine jars. The main deck collapsed. Eventually the hull broke open and dishes and amphoras spilled out in all directions. Sand and mud drifted down from above and gradually covered the ship. Boulders from the island fell upon it. Finally, when the ship was completely buried, it was preserved from further destruction. By the year 1952, when Cousteau began his excavation, there was nothing to be seen but a mound on the sea floor, marked by amphoras and broken dishes. The vessel might have remained in this condition for another thousand years had it not been for the observation of the salvage diver and his taste for lobsters.

The divers stood around eagerly as Professor Benoît confirmed his first identification of the pottery brought up by Cousteau. Then, in a scurry for masks and tanks, they tumbled overboard and finned downward to the wreck. A wire basket was lowered and filled. Jars and dishes were brought up encrusted with clinging oysters, sponges, mussels, and branches of red and yellow coral.

In the first days Cousteau was under the impression that he and his crew could clear the site in two months. He intended to bring everything up, including the ship. Just as at Mahdia, he put his divers on seventeen-minute shifts. At the 140-foot depth this was the maximum time they could spend under water without a long period for decompression. Again as at Mahdia, a rifle shot fired into the water recalled the divers to the ship.

However, the beginning was deceptively easy. Although the top material was loose by far the greatest part seemed to be embedded in cement. In order to attack it a large suction pipe was lowered. It was so powerful that the divers literally vacuumed away the matrix of the mound. Large objects were loosened and dug out by hand. Smaller ones were sucked up into the pipe, and ejected along with water and debris into a filter basket on the island. Above water the pipe ran along the derrick and under the engine house to its outlet on the far side of Grand Congloué. This prevented the dirt discharged from muddying the water around the wreck. It was several months before the pit was deep and wide enough to reveal the hull and ribs of the Greek vessel.

All during this time the *Calypso* had been the base of operations. The ship was often in real danger of being dashed against the cliffs. With winter coming on and the prospect of more frequent storms Cousteau decided to transfer his excavation headquarters to the island itself.

The French government came to his aid by sending a crew of engineers. They blasted a platform on the cliff and installed a winch to lift the finds from the wreck. An eighty-foot boom was anchored on the island to carry the suction pipe out over the wreck, and an air compressor was installed to power the suction pipe. With ten divers housed in United States surplus Nissen huts, work was resumed, and the French flag was raised over Port Calypso. By now everyone knew that the excavation would take many months. It actually took a total of six years.

News of the unusual excavation brought Cousteau all kinds of assistance. The Marseille Chamber of Commerce adopted the islanders, and sent them an electric light plant. By May of 1953 the crew reached the keel of the ship.

Later that year Cousteau tested a new idea in underwater archaeology and found it very useful. An underwater television camera in a steel barrel sent pictures over a cable to two television sets in the *Calypso*. This permitted the two resident archaeologists, Ferdinand Lallemand and Henri Médan, who had joined the expedition but who were not divers, to direct the underwater activities from first-hand observation.

Some seven thousand amphoras and ten thousand bowls, cups, and flasks were finally recovered from the wreck. The divers brought up sheets of lead plating from the hull and deck and thousands of small copper nails, which had been coated with lead and used to fasten the plating to the ship. They found numerous iron tools, one lead sculpture which may have been the figurehead, and the anchor. They also found many yards of lead pipe, about three inches in diameter with joint holes drilled in it. The archaeologists still have not decided whether it was part of a pumping system or represented the captain's personal plumbing.

Finally Cousteau had to abandon his hope of raising the entire ship. When uncovered, the old wood of the hull had a rubbery texture, though it appeared sound. Brought to the surface and exposed to the air, however, it was found to be tunneled with shipworms, and unless coated immediately with a preservative it shrank to about one-third its original size. Since Cousteau could think of no practical way of preserving the huge ship he had to give up his dream of salvaging it.

The archaeologists' careful analysis of the evidence given them by the divers and their later study of the wreck on the underwater television screen enabled them to construct the story of the accident, as we have read it. They also put together the

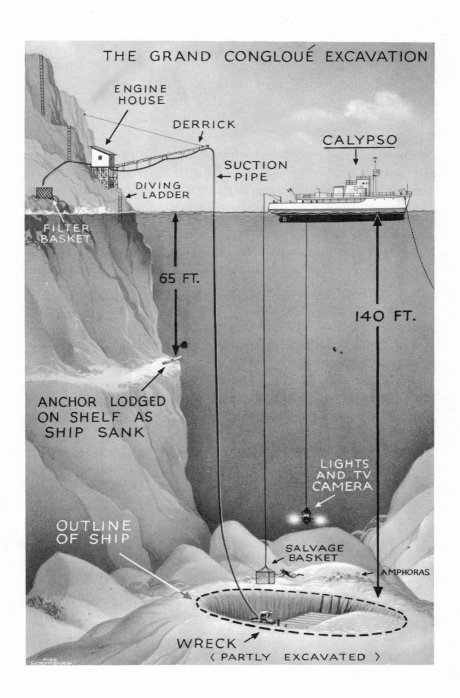

THE GRAND CONGLOUÉ EXCAVATION

ENGINE HOUSE

DERRICK

CALYPSO

SUCTION PIPE

DIVING LADDER

FILTER BASKET

65 FT.

140 FT.

ANCHOR LODGED ON SHELF AS SHIP SANK

LIGHTS AND TV CAMERA

OUTLINE OF SHIP

SALVAGE BASKET

AMPHORAS

WRECK
⟨ PARTLY EXCAVATED ⟩

description of the Grand Congloué vessel. The order in which the pottery and wine jars were stowed in the hold told them her itinerary and port of origin. Little by little they sorted the evidence for information about Greek shipbuilding techniques and navigational knowledge. But the prize bit of detective work must be credited to Professor Benoît.

Many amphoras from the wreck had the mark SES along with an anchor or trident pressed into their rims. Supposing that SES must stand for the man who owned the sunken ship, Benoît looked through museum collections and Roman writings until he found references to a third-century merchant shipowner named Marcus Sestius. Not only had Sestius lived at the same time as the wreck, but he came from the Greek island of Dēlos. This, judging from the type of Greek wine jar on board, was the vessel's most likely port of origin. Another detail from the life of Sestius was found by French archaeologists excavating at Dēlos. They uncovered a stone slab, which had inscribed on it Greek words to the effect that the Roman merchant, Marcus Sestius, had been made an honorary citizen of the island in the year 240 B.C.

Little did the unfortunate Marcus Sestius imagine that he would be remembered by history because of a fortune lost and a ship which went to the bottom of the sea.

9

Water, Water Everywhere

AT least one plunder ship that left Greece laden with antique art treasures was not Roman. It sank off the Greek isle of Kýthēra in comparatively modern times. In it were the now famous "Elgin marbles."

Thomas Bruce, the seventh Earl of Elgin, was sent to Constantinople as the British Ambassador to Turkey in 1799. The Turks were then in possession of Greece and had been for almost three hundred and fifty years. Lord Elgin considered it his duty to visit Athens and check on the condition of the ruins. What he found at the Acropolis shocked him.

The Acropolis is a group of majestic Greek buildings which stands on a hill in the southern part of Athens. Its crowning splendor, the Parthenon, is considered to be the most perfect and impressive example of Greek architecture. Until 1687 the Parthenon stood almost intact. In that year the Turks, who were at war with the Venetians, used it to store their gunpowder. A direct hit by a Venetian artilleryman blew off the roof. After that the ruins were used as a convenient source of building stone and were in the process of being dismantled when the British Ambassador arrived on the scene.

Elgin went right to work. His first plan was to make casts and drawings of all the marble sculptures. Later he received permission from the Turks to remove all the stones with inscriptions. He ended by removing from the Parthenon all the sculptures he could take without causing structural damage.

At one time he even thought of taking a whole Greek temple, but settled at last for a single column.

The material was packed in sixteen huge cases for shipment to England on the brig *Mentor*. The *Mentor* took the same course as the Roman plunder ship that sank at Antikÿthēra two thousand years earlier. It ran into a storm, was blown off course, and finally had to take shelter at Kÿthēra island, just north of Antikÿthēra. In spite of all precautions it crashed on the rocks and sank. All those aboard managed to escape, but the priceless collection went to the bottom of the sea.

When Elgin heard the news he was appalled at the thought of what he had done. He had gone to great efforts to save these masterpieces of antiquity only to lose them to the sea. His only hope lay in the possibility that they might be salvaged. The hope was slim, but it had some merit. The *Mentor* had sunk in only sixty feet of water.

The technical problem of salvaging the treasure was put into the hands of Elgin's capable secretary, Mr. W. R. Hamilton. Hamilton's first thought was to hire a professional salvor, and for this purpose he looked up a burly Italian ship captain from La Spezia named Basilio Menachini. Menachini's reward for raising the treasure in three months was to be appointed British vice-consul of La Spezia. Before the Italian could carry out the contract the Greek war of independence began in earnest, and Hamilton's well-laid plans were cast aside. Some months later Hamilton secured instead the services of a group of divers from the island of Samos. They worked diligently and by 1804, two years after the wreck, every one of the cases of sculpture had been recovered.

Each case, as soon as it was recovered, was hurriedly taken to shore and buried under brushwood, stones, and seaweed. Hamilton was in constant fear that the priceless marble sculptures might be stolen by pirates.

It was 1809 before all of the Elgin marbles reached England. Although Elgin had spent 70,000 British pounds out of his own pocket on this venture, the British government paid him only half of this amount. He saw his treasure put on display in the British Museum, only to find that he was severely criticized by many people for having ruined the Parthenon.

It is hard to say whether Lord Elgin was wrong in removing the sculptures from their original setting. However, if he had not taken them it is very likely that they would have been claimed by some other nation or destroyed during the Greek war of independence.

There was, among the Caesars of Imperial Rome, one known as Gaius Caesar and nicknamed Caligula. This strange man, sometimes insanely cruel, sometimes supremely ridiculous, had a short but turbulent reign from 37 to 41 A.D. Before his untimely death at the hands of his followers he completed many grandiose projects. One of them was the construction of two magnificent ships, which were never destined to sail the ocean waves. Instead they floated serenely upon the quiet waters of Lake Nemi, seventeen miles southeast of Rome. They were built as temples and dedicated to the cult of Diana, the goddess of the lake. Caligula used them for his personal pleasure and recreation, except for the few days in August when the cult of the goddess was celebrated. He adorned them with priceless artistic treasures.

For nineteen hundred years the galleys lay at the bottom of Lake Nemi, beneath sixteen to sixty-nine feet of water. Their existence was well known, and throughout the centuries several attempts were made to salvage them. The Italian dictator Mussolini succeeded where others had failed. He simply ordered that the lake be drained. It was emptied, through an underground channel originally made during the reign of the Emperor Claudius, into the vale of Aricia. The prodigious task of pumping the lake took four years. The pumps began working on October 20, 1928, and by November, 1932, one ship had been installed in a hangar and the other was exposed in

ONE OF CALIGULA'S SHIPS ON LAKE NEMI

the mud on shore. For the first and only time two ships of classical antiquity were put on display to be examined and admired by archaeologists.

The vessels were in amazingly good condition, since fresh water has none of the destructive crustaceans of the sea. They were huge, according to ancient standards. Shallow of draft and broad in the beam, one measured 68 by 234 feet, the other 78 by 239 feet. The superstructures had been destroyed during the earlier attempts at salvage, but one structure with copper tiles was recognized as the roof of a deck cabin. The sides of the ships were encrusted with gold. Their hulls were made of several different kinds of wood, protected by leaden plates held in position with copper nails.

In 1943 these noble ships became the victims of war. They were burned by the Germans during the Italian campaign of

World War II. Fortunately most of their artistic treasures were preserved in a museum built to house them at Lake Nemi.

There is always a certain amount of danger to diving in strange waters. It is hazardous to explore the dark and winding passages of an unknown cave on foot. But imagine, if you will, what it is like to dive into cold, black waters deep in the bowels of the earth, not knowing when or where you will again breathe fresh air or see the light of day. A French cave explorer by the name of Norbert Casteret did just that, and found some of the oldest sculptures ever made by man.

It was in August, 1922, that Casteret first came to the village of Montespan in the Pyrenees mountains of southern France. He had heard of the Grotto of Montespan and wanted to explore it for signs of prehistoric cave art and relics. Knowing the geology of the region well he concluded that the cave had been formed by an underground river eating its way through the porous limestone rock. He was sure that the grotto had been dry at the end of the last Ice Age, when the hairy mammoth roamed the earth and men sought shelter from the cold in caves.

In order to enter the cave Casteret had to squeeze through a hole barely larger than his own body. He found himself in a cavern ten to thirteen feet wide and from six to ten feet high. At the far end was an underground river. Here the ceiling dipped and the floor plunged below the water level.

Casteret was alone. He had told no one he was going, and he knew that if anything happened to him there would be no rescue. He carried no special equipment. However, he was an experienced cave explorer. The memory of previous explorations and his own obstinacy urged him on. Holding his breath he plunged into the water and came up a few feet beyond in a hidden cave. He was in pitch blackness, but he could breathe fresh air and he sensed that the cave was large. Fearful of losing his sense of direction he turned back.

When Casteret entered the cave the following day he carried with him candles and matches in a watertight case. Once again he swam through the submerged passage. He lit a candle and followed the cave. His progress was stopped when the ceiling again dipped into the water. By now Casteret had gone too far to think of retreating. He was sure he was near the outlet of the cave. Once again he drew a deep breath and swam down into the unknown. Following the roof of the cave with his fingertips, he emerged a minute later in still another cold, dark passage.

Even with his great experience his mind was filled with misgivings. He knew that the slightest accident, like losing or wetting his matches, could be fatal. His footprints were the only signposts for the way back. After hours of struggling along on slippery clay banks, squeezing through narrow passages, his body numbed from the cold water he reached the end of the cave. Above him, through a small cleft in the rock, came a faint glow of light. The incoming water held the warmth of the sun, but the hole was too small for Casteret. He had to return the way he came.

Although Casteret found no evidence of prehistoric man on his first visits to the Grotto there were still many passages to investigate. He decided to continue his explorations the following year with his friend, Henri Godin.

The summer of 1923 was a dry one in France. When the two men arrived in Montespan they found the water level in the cave much lower than in the previous season. They dived through the first underwater passage, but instead of forcing the second chose to follow a dry tunnel. Casteret found what he thought was a promising spot and began to dig with a small pick. Almost at once he was rewarded by a chipped flint, sure evidence that prehistoric man had been there before him. He lifted his candle to examine the walls. Then suddenly he stopped, awestruck. Before him was the life-size clay figure of a bear. It sat, crouching on a pedestal, as it had sat for twenty thousand years. The young explorer wondered if he had stumbled upon the oldest statue in the world.

Casteret shouted to Godin, who came running to join him. Spellbound, the two men traversed the length of the cavern. Revealed in the flickering light of their candles was a primeval circus. Engraved horses trotted across the walls. One bore the brand of a human hand on its flank. A wide-eyed bison ogled them from across the centuries. Behind it lumbered a hairy mammoth. A deer leaped away in fright, followed by a wild goat, and a hyena skulked in the shadows. Mingled with the animal engravings were carved symbols, their mystic meanings lost in time.

Casteret shined the light of the candle on the floor. Cold chills shot down his spine, as he recognized a human footprint that was not his own. All about him he discerned the intermin-

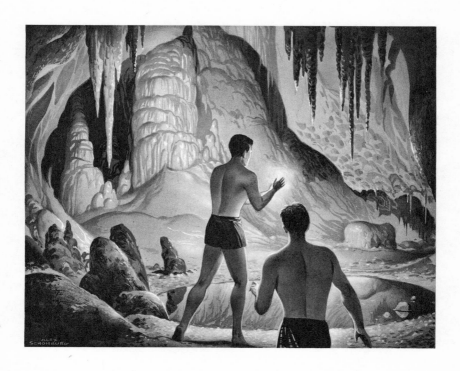

gled prints of bear claws and naked human feet. Had men fought here with bears, he wondered? Or had they danced with bear claws fastened to their feet? Incredibly the prints had remained undisturbed for two hundred centuries.

Casteret and Godin returned for a closer look at the clay bear. The proof of its antiquity was a scaly encrustation of calcite, deposited through the centuries by water dripping from the roof of the cave. The head of the bear was missing. In its place was the remains of a wooden peg. Between the sculptured forepaws lay the fossilized skull of a bear cub. The body was scarred as if it had been struck many times by stone spears. Casteret guessed that at one time the image had been covered with a bearskin and head. Probably spears had been thrown at it, as a form of magic to insure a successful hunt.

As the explorers left the cave they felt strangely privileged, for they had pushed aside the barrier of time. This dark cavern, hidden from prying, curious eyes, had been the scene of Stone Age rites. Who knows, they asked themselves, what mysteries the clay bear witnessed in the dawn of prehistory?

On the southwest coast of Turkey there are many islands. Sometime about 1400 B.C. a small merchant ship tried to pass between two of them, cracked up against the jagged rocks, and sank in ninety feet of water. It was discovered in 1959 by Peter Throckmorton, a photo-journalist from New York City. When his preliminary investigations showed that it was the oldest ship so far found under water, dating to the Late Bronze Age, he notified the Council for Underwater Archaeology in San Francisco. The Council in turn asked the University Museum of the University of Pennsylvania if they would be interested in organizing an expedition. The answer was an enthusiastic "Yes!"

The excavation got under way in June, 1960, under the direction of George Bass, a diving archaeologist from the University Museum. The crew set themselves a grueling schedule in order to complete the work before the winter storms began in September. Beneath the deck cargo of copper ingots they found deck planking and the remains of reed baskets. In what they believed to be the captain's quarters they recovered four Egyptian scarabs with hieroglyphic inscriptions, a set of "apothecary's weights," a lamp, a very fine Syrian cylinder seal, and a polished stone macehead. They even uncovered the remains of the crew's last meal and some white powder was identified as tin oxide. Apparently the captain was making his own bronze as he sailed along. In another section of the ship they found thousands of glass beads, evidently part of the trading material. When all the results of the excavation are analyzed, we will know much more about this ship that sailed the seas so very long ago.

Many ancient shipwrecks have been reported along the coasts of the Mediterranean Sea. An Etruscan ship wrecked near the Cap d'Antibes on the coast of southern France sometime during the sixth century B.C. awaits excavation. When it is investigated it will surely yield much needed information about the Etruscans, the mysterious people who established the first true civilization in Italy over 2,500 years ago.

Most of these discoveries have been accidents. In Piraeus harbor, the port of the city of Athens, an ancient flat-bottomed transport ship was discovered during dredging operations in 1930. Apparently it had caught fire and sunk, as it was lying in port ready to set sail for Italy. The load of two-thousand-year-old carved marble sculptures and reliefs was perfectly preserved by its covering of thick harbor slime.

The family of Greek gods was ruled by Zeus. This greatest of all gods is the subject of the finest Greek bronze statue in existence. The magnificent work is that of a master sculptor of the Golden Age, the fifth century B.C. He is depicted in heroic scale, his arms and legs outspread, ready to hurl a thunder bolt. The statue has come to be known as the "Thundering Zeus."

The left arm of the statue was discovered by sponge divers, while fishing in the sound between the Greek coasts of Thessaly and Cape Artémision. They took it to local archaeologists, who were immediately impressed with the perfection of the workmanship. In 1928 an archaeological excavation led by George Karo of the German Archaeological Institute in Athens was organized under the sponsorship of Alexander Benakis, a leading Greek art patron, and the Greek navy.

For a while the excavation promised to be a great success. The divers brought up the rest of the statue, and it turned out to be of even finer quality than the archaeologists had hoped. They also recovered parts of another bronze masterpiece, a rearing race horse held by a tiny jockey or stable boy. Then an unfortunate accident put a sudden halt to the project.

Greek sponge divers are an independent lot and do not like to be told how to handle themselves in the water, especially by those they consider amateurs. Although provided with the most modern helmet diving suits available at the time the divers preferred to use their own well-worn and outdated equipment. They also refused to pay attention to the decompression tables. It was their custom to gauge depth and time underwater by their own lifetime of experience. However, the depth at Cape Artémision was considerably below their usual working level. One diver, particularly scornful of the scientists and their advice to rise slowly and at intervals, decided to prove his point. He surged up rapidly from 140 feet, laughed uproariously at his more cautious companions, and then fell dead before their horrified eyes, the victim of explosive decompression. After this tragedy the superstitious divers were reluctant to return to the wreck, and the excavation was stopped.

Today, if you visit the United Nations building in New York City you can see in the main lobby a cast of this statue of almighty Zeus brandishing a thunderbolt. It was given by Greece to the family of nations. There is no more fitting tribute to underwater archaeology.

Fishermen are constantly hauling up relics from shipwrecks in their nets. Unfortunately, because their nets are dragged over miles of sea bottom, they can rarely pinpoint the exact spot of discovery.

Since 1925 Italian fishermen from the town of Albenga had been getting amphoras along with their fish. It seemed fairly obvious that a large underwater deposit existed, but it was many years before the site was investigated. This was the first and probably the only time when commercial salvage equipment, such as that used to recover the cargoes of modern steel ships, was used for an underwater excavation.

In 1950 Professor Nino Lamboglia, director of the archaeological organization known as the Italian Institute of Ligurian Studies, persuaded Commandant Quaglia, a professional salvage expert, to loan him his salvage ship, *Artiglio II,* for twelve days. Quaglia anchored over the Albenga fishing grounds. A diver was sent down to investigate and reported finding an ancient wreck at a depth of 120 feet. The accumulation of amphoras, cemented together with marine life, was distributed over an area 45 by 150 feet. The outlines of the ship were still plainly visible. Apparently it had been the same size as those found at Mahdia and Anthéor. The "grab," huge jaws of steel designed to pull apart riveted steel plating, crunched into the rotted timbers and brought them, along with clumps of amphoras, to the deck of the *Artiglio II.* The work was directed by a man in an underwater observation chamber. No divers were used and no photographs were taken. In spite of the hundreds of amphoras hauled out of the sea the excavation was not successful from an archaeological point of view. The crude methods used resulted in the loss of too much valuable information. Lamboglia admitted his mistake. He had found through sad experience that in archaeology nothing ever replaces the need for well-trained human hands and minds. It was discovered, however, that the ship, like others of its period, was sheathed in lead. It was carrying a load of wine and oil from southern Italy to France or Spain, when it sank during the first half of the first century B.C.

Not all shipwrecks have been found in the Mediterranean. Norwegian diver-archaeologists have examined seven Viking ships discovered in 1959 near Frederikssund, Denmark. They were remarkably well preserved, and dated from about the year 940 A.D.

One of the most amazing shipwrecks is that of the *Vasa*. It sank in the harbor of Stockholm, Sweden, in August, 1628. This flagship of the Royal Swedish navy was a magnificent example of seventeenth-century naval might. Along the hull from the prow to the poop deck were gilded and brightly-painted carvings. As it prepared to leave on its maiden voyage a great crowd assembled to admire it and to wish its crew well. The red doors of the gun ports were drawn up, so that all could see the golden lion heads with their red tongues and bared fangs carved on the undersides.

The moment arrived and the *Vasa*, its sails billowing in the wind, moved slowly out of port. No sooner had it left the harbor than a sharp gust of wind swept down the steep rock on the southern shore and hit the ship almost straight across. The *Vasa* listed heavily to one side. Water poured through the open gun ports, and the ship, its flags still flying, sank scarcely one hundred yards from the horrified spectators on shore.

In the years that followed, several attempts were made to salvage the guns and pay chest. Thirty years after the tragedy a Swedish engineer, Lieutenant Colonel Hans Albrecht von Treileben, used diving bells, and successfully recovered more than fifty cannon. With this the salvage operations were closed and the *Vasa* was forgotten.

It wasn't until 1920, when several unidentified cannon were

found in Stockholm harbor, that the investigations were re-opened. A Swedish historian, Professor Ahnlund, discovered accounts of the disaster among some old legal documents. Then, in 1954, a Stockholm wreck enthusiast named Anders Franzén began a systematic search for the *Vasa*.

Franzén was no diver. He designed an instrument with which he could bring samples of wood from the bottom to where he sat in a small rowboat. Nothing of value turned up the first two summers, but in 1956 Franzén collected several pieces of black oak from a hump the size of the *Vasa*. He reported the discovery to the National Maritime Museum and they in turn made contact with the Swedish navy. E. P. Fälting, an ace navy diver, was sent to investigate.

Diving down through the cold, clear waters of Stockholm harbor Fälting landed almost on top of a wreck the size of a large warship. The big oaken hull stood upright and intact. He shot back to the surface to tell Franzén the good news.

Since then many exploratory dives have been made under the direction of Commander Edward Clason of the Royal Swedish navy. The ship's identity was definitely established in 1958, when a cannon was recovered bearing the crest of the Vasa dynasty.

The *Vasa's* unusually good state of preservation can be explained by the very cold, brackish water in which it lay. The marine life which ordinarily destroys a wooden ship cannot live in the Baltic Sea. Commander Clason's group of helmet and Aqualung divers from the Navy Experimental Diving Unit now believe they can raise and float the *Vasa*. They plan to continue their exploration of the hulk. Then cables will be fitted under the ship and it will be moved to shallow water for repair before being refloated. If their plan succeeds the *Vasa* may once again attract a throng of admirers.

10

Cities under the Sea

CITIES under the sea! It is almost impossible to think of underwater archaeology without imagining sunken cities.

What visions these words bring to mind! We picture ghostly palaces abandoned to the fish and seaweed. Long avenues of crumbling houses stretch out in our imagination and fade again into the murky twilight of the sea. Stories of sunken cities intrigue us as they have intrigued the minds of men for thousands of years. One of the first and most persistent legends is that of the lost continent of Atlantis.

More than 2,300 years ago the Greek philosopher Plato wrote about an island in the Atlantic Ocean that lay directly beyond the Pillars of Hercules. Here men lived an ideal way of life. The land was happy, prosperous, and well governed. The kings of Atlantis ruled most of Africa and Europe, but when they set out to conquer Greece they were opposed by armies of Athenian soldiers. A great battle was fought and the Atlanteans were defeated by the men of Athens. When the victory was complete and the conquering Greeks came to Atlantis to collect the spoils of war a catastrophe occurred. Earthquakes rocked the land. The sea rose up and flooded the countryside. Then, as Plato wrote, "the whole Greek army in one evil day and in one evil night sank into the earth, and the island of Atlantis sank into the ocean and was seen no more."

Ever since Plato, people have been arguing over the story of the lost Atlantis. If the island of Atlantis ever existed, it should be possible to locate it. If located, it could be excavated. The problem is interesting enough to warrant a careful examination of the legend, and some of the theories about it that have been formulated.

Plato tells us that the Greeks themselves had no records of a battle between Atlanteans and Athenians, nor of the catastrophe that followed. He claimed to have heard the story from Egyptian priests. According to Egyptian tradition Atlantis disappeared below the waves about 7000 B.C., some six thousand years before the beginning of Grecian civilization. If this is accepted as true it is hard to imagine how the Atlanteans could possibly have fought a war with the Athenians.

Over the years there have been more than twenty-five thousand articles and books written on the subject of Atlantis. One of the more absurd theories suggested is that Atlantis was a part of the earth that broke loose and whirled off into space to become the moon. Geologists tell us, however, that the moon was formed billions of years ago, long before there were men on earth.

When the impressive ruined cities of the Aztec and Maya Indians of Central America were rediscovered in the middle of the last century the Atlantis legend had a great revival. "Could these noble temples have been built by primitive Indians?" it was asked. Since at that time there was no scientific evidence available to the contrary it was concluded that they were built by refugees from Atlantis, who reached the western hemisphere after the destruction of their island.

This theory had a short life. Soon afterward some of the documents written during and after the Spanish conquest of Mexico and Central America were discovered in archives in Spain. In them were detailed descriptions of the highly-advanced Indian civilizations existing at the time of the discovery of America. Later, when archaeologists began to excavate the ruins, they found abundant evidence to prove that the Indian civilizations were deeply rooted in the western hemisphere. They found no indication that they could have originated or even been influenced by Europe or the lost Atlantis.

A more logical explanation of Atlantis is that the legend really refers to the island of Crete. The Egyptians carried on a lively trade with Cretan merchants, who sailed to their shores. When the Cretans were conquered by the Greeks the trade stopped abruptly. To the Egyptians, so far away, it may have seemed as though the island had sunk suddenly into the sea.

Most people today are content to regard the story as a myth created by Plato himself. But myths die hard. There are those who argue that Atlantis still lies beneath the waters of the Atlantic. However, in spite of all the words, the heated arguments, and the fanciful theories, all scientific evidence is weighted heavily against the legend of Atlantis. Geologists and oceanographers have made careful examinations of the part of the Atlantic sea bed where Atlantis was supposed to have existed. Their studies show that the ocean floor has lain undisturbed for 500,000,000 years. The Atlantic ridge, a range of underwater mountains, does show signs of having once been above the surface of the sea. This, however, was in a remote geologic epoch, when mankind had not yet come into being.

Another myth that persists is that of the sunken kingdom of Ys. According to French legends, it once existed off the coast of Brittany, but sank into the sea sometime in the fifth century A.D. The French are fond of their legend and insist that on certain occasions they can hear the bells of the sunken cathedral. Although numerous attempts have been made to locate Ys no trace of the drowned city has been found. There is no doubt the fanciful stories of Ys are largely myth. However, the sea floor off the coast of Brittany is a jungle of seaweed. It would be difficult to locate ruins of a sunken city, if one did exist.

The Greek city of Helice on the north shore of the Peloponnesus is an historical city under the sea. It was destroyed by a disastrous earthquake in the winter of 373 B.C.

According to the historian Diodorus Siculus, who lived during the first century B.C.:

> The blow came at night, so that when the houses crashed and crumbled under the force of the shock, the population, owing to the darkness and to the surprise and bewilderment occasioned by the event, had no power to struggle for life. The majority were caught in the falling houses and annihilated, but as day returned some survivors dashed from the ruins and, when they thought they had escaped the danger, met with a greater and still more incredible disaster. For the sea rose to a vast new height, and a wave towering even higher washed away and drowned all the inhabitants and their native lands as well.

The disaster was explained by many as the wrath of the old sea god Poseidon. He was angry, they believed, because the townspeople of Helice had failed to respect him and to make sacrifices before his sacred altars.

In 1950 four French divers joined archaeologists of the French Archaeological School at Athens, Greece, to plan an underwater investigation of the sunken city. The project ended in complete failure. The water was so muddy that the visibility was almost zero. Two nearby rivers discharged a constant flow of silt, and the underwater terrain was a plain of mud, broken only by an occasional deep chasm. There was not a trace of Helice.

In recent years the Greek archaeologist, Spyridon Marinatos, has carried out an extensive survey of the region around ancient Helice and now feels he is truly on the track of the buried city. And buried it may well be, rather than submerged! Historical records indicate that the city was never very far from shore. On the other hand geologists and local farmers claim that deposits of river mud extend the coastlines almost three feet a year, thus burying Helice deeper and deeper. Marinatos has calculated that by now the remains of the city must lie beneath dry land, some distance inland from the present shore. Unfortunately, even with modern methods and equipment the excavation of the ruins would be a gigantic and costly procedure. Although the land above Helice may be quite dry there is no doubt that the ruins lie below the water table. The archaeological investigation would still have to be conducted underwater. Nevertheless Helice may in time be excavated. When it is, its importance will overshadow even that of the famous buried city of Pompeii and shed new light on life during the Golden Age of Greece.

On the desolate, marshy shore of Fos-sur-Mer on the south coast of France archaeologists conducted an underwater excavation of a drowned Roman villa. The work began in 1948 and lasted four years.

The name Fos-sur-Mer means ditch on the sea. Historical records and local traditions indicate that the Roman general Marius built the city about the year 100 B.C., and dug a canal to link the Mediterranean Sea with the River Rhône. For his city Marius chose a little village that had been in existence since the Bronze Age.

During the Roman period Fos grew into a thriving seaport. Not only did it offer access to the River Rhône, but it was at the intersection of three roads that ran north, east, and west through France. There was a constant and busy flow of sea and land traffic. At this time one of the townspeople built a villa by the seashore. Unquestionably he was wealthy, for the villa was not the sort an ordinary man could afford. Very likely he was a shipmaster, a local Gaul, who had accepted the customs and citizenship of Rome.

At the end of the Roman period Fos began to decline. Many of the merchants and shipowners moved their homes and businesses to nearby Marseille. By the Middle Ages there was nothing left of the city but a little fishing harbor. During the centuries that followed a gradual geologic change took place. The land sank and the sea rose to cover it. The mouths of the Rhône shifted, and silt from the river spread over the drowned houses of Fos.

In the twentieth century Fos-sur-Mer became a summer playground for vacationing families from Marseille. Divers exploring the seashore discovered fragments of Roman architecture, and reported them to the local archaeological society. The French archaeologist, Dr. Beaucaire, was immediately fascinated with prospects of an underwater excavation. There are many monumental Roman ruins in southern France, but no Roman houses. These were destroyed by their owners centuries ago, as styles in architecture changed. To find a Roman villa, protected and preserved from the ravages of time by a covering of mud and water, would be finding missing pages from the book of history. Dr. Beaucaire planned his first underwater excavation with the same care and precision he had exhibited in directing excavations on dry land. As a result it became a model for future undersea archaeological operations.

Dr. Beaucaire's team of volunteer undersea explorers were men already well trained in dry land archaeology. An area was measured off, extending from ten yards to five hundred yards offshore. Here the water was marshy, and ranged in depth from three to fifteen feet. The searchers' first task was to lift the top layer of sand. Beneath this they found a deposit of thin, sticky clay, thirty inches deep. Finally, with great elation, they found the walls of a Roman villa.

It was no easy excavation. Picks and shovels were used below the water line. Quantities of sand, pebbles, and mud had to be moved. Many cubic yards of soil were sieved, in order to recover tiny items that would otherwise have been missed. A Roman house altar surrounded by clay lamps was discovered within the ruined walls of the villa. The mud had preserved even the smallest objects. Among the artifacts were numerous household utensils such as cheese molds and drinking cups.

These objects are now on display in a small museum in Fos. A study of them revealed a picture of domestic life in a provincial Roman settlement. The sea had preserved a period in history that the land had long ago destroyed.

Coming closer to American shores we find the story of Port Royal, the main port on the island of Jamaica, since 1655 a British possession in the West Indies. During the 1600's Port Royal was reputed to be the most wicked city in the world. Its inhabitants were of many nationalities, but they had one thing in common. Virtually every one was a fugitive from the law. Not only was Port Royal the center of the slave trade, it was

the haven of pirates and buccaneers. It reached the height of its fame during the heyday of the pirate Henry Morgan. He used the fine harbor and well-fortified shores as a convenient base of operations from which he sallied forth to sack and pillage Spanish cities throughout the Caribbean.

In spite of its beautiful setting Port Royal was a squalid, ugly city. It was built entirely on a narrow, sandy spit of land that extended into the sea. Even the two- to four-story brick buildings that crowded the center of the town were built on foundations of loose gravel. Frame shacks and bamboo huts clung to the outskirts.

The end came dramatically on June 7, 1692. Shortly before noon the earth began to heave and rock. The first earthquake

EARTHQUAKE AND TIDAL WAVE AT PORT ROYAL · JUNE 7, 1692

was followed almost immediately by a second and then a third. Thousands of panic-stricken people milled through the streets, seeking refuge but not knowing where to flee. A crowd of men, women, and children gathered in the Church of St. Paul to pray, but their prayers changed to screams as the huge bell tower crashed into their midst. From afar came the rumble of mountain avalanches. The sky turned a dull and reddish color. Crevices opened suddenly in the earth, swallowing people and houses. Then came a new terror.

A tidal wave formed and rolled in from the sea. It toppled the boats in the harbor and surged over the city. One ship, the *Swan Frigot,* was carried by the gigantic wave over the tops of the houses of Port Royal. Those on board miraculously escaped injury.

When the sun rose the following morning it illuminated a scene of desolation. Two-thirds of Port Royal had disappeared forever beneath the sea, and more than two thousand of its residents had lost their lives.

In the years that followed, Port Royal made a feeble return to life, but it never regained its former importance. Instead, the government headquarters and most of the port activities were moved to higher and more stable ground. The new capital was named Kingstown.

For years the fishermen of Jamaica have delighted in telling imaginative stories to tourists about the fabulous drowned city of Port Royal. They have pointed out the spot where on clear days one supposedly can see the top of the church bell tower. It matters little to them that the tower was destroyed in 1692.

One well-known diver and sea adventurer claimed to have found the old city completely intact beneath the waves, and a movie was based on his tale. In spite of his fabulous stories, however, he was unable to produce even one historical artifact. Other divers, exploring the area soon learned why. Below Port Royal's green, silt-laden waters lay a bottom of thick, soft mud, completely hiding from sight any trace of the ruined city.

Among the divers who came to look were the amateur underwater archaeologists Ed Link and his wife Marion. In their converted shrimp boat, *Sea Diver,* they had already explored many shipwrecks in the Gulf of Mexico and in the Caribbean, and had the practical experience that their predecessors lacked. However, even they were discouraged by the impenetrable mud bottom. On an exploratory visit to Port Royal in 1956 they dug a trench with a small dredge and penetrated four to six feet before finding traces of walls.

When they returned three years later they were fully prepared to undertake the task of excavating the drowned city. The old *Sea Diver* had been turned in for a luxurious new model, equipped from the keel up for underwater archaeology. The captain, Ed Link, was also the designer. Before devoting himself to a search for history under the sea Mr. Link was the inventor of numerous electronic and aeronautical devices. He made a fortune with his best-known invention, the Link Trainer, a device used to teach beginning pilots the conditions of flight and battle without their having to leave the ground. Putting his fertile mind to work Link designed a diving and salvage ship that could meet even the challenge of Port Royal. Partly jet-propelled and fully equipped with radar, sonar, automatic pilot, and gyrocompass, it also had two large generators. The electricity powered a compressor large enough to provide air for many divers, and to operate a ten-inch-diameter air lift and heavy-duty jetting hose. Both the air lift and the jet hose were powerful enough to clear away the heavy covering of silt and gravel at Port Royal. Heavy booms and electric winches were mounted on the deck.

The Links' excavation began in June, 1959, with a crew of twelve aboard the *Sea Diver.* The project was jointly sponsored by the National Geographic Society, the Smithsonian Institution, and the Institute of Jamaica. There were funds to support it only for ten weeks.

Ed Link prepared a chart of old Port Royal, which he carefully compared with existing landmarks. This chart, in addition to the original property deeds which were found on file at the Record Office in nearby Spanish Town, made it possible for him to plot the underwater location of the streets and buildings. Logically the first step of the actual excavation was to test the chart with a sonar survey. Link marked on it any abrupt variations in the soundings, on the assumption that they indicated the remains of old buildings.

For the first trial Link chose a complex of buildings marked on his chart as the king's warehouses. They were chosen because of their size and because they probably housed valuable merchandise. However, after several days in which nothing but mud and gravel was brought up by the air lift Link decided to move to a new location. After a careful study of the chart he chose a spot close to the east wall of Fort James, the old British fort at the entrance to the harbor. Here the crew recovered a quantity of artifacts, all suggesting that the divers were digging in a kitchen. One group of five pots was just as it had stood in the fireplace: two large brass pots, two iron ones, and a small ceramic pot with a handle. Since the murky water limited visibility most of the specimens were located with the aid of an underwater metal detector.

The Smithsonian Institution marine archaeologist, Mendel Peterson, checked the chart and concluded that the kitchen had belonged to a man named James Littleton. It was used to supply either Fort James or a nearby tavern, and was equipped to serve large numbers of people. At Port Royal, as elsewhere in the Caribbean, kitchens were often set apart in separate buildings.

Moving from this spot to another just off the customs dock, a different discovery was made. From the number and kind of tools salvaged, Peterson and Link identified the site as the shop of a ship dealer. The owner must have fancied old guns. A fifteenth-century Spanish swivel gun, a hundred years old at the time of the earthquake, was found.

The most interesting discovery rocketed out of the air lift one day amid the usual load of gravel and mud. It glinted briefly in the sun and was snatched by an alert diver. Examination revealed it to be an elegant brass watch in a remarkable state of preservation. A layer of coral covering the face was carefully removed. Beneath it the silver Roman numerals on the face were distinctly visible and the delicate brass gears inside were

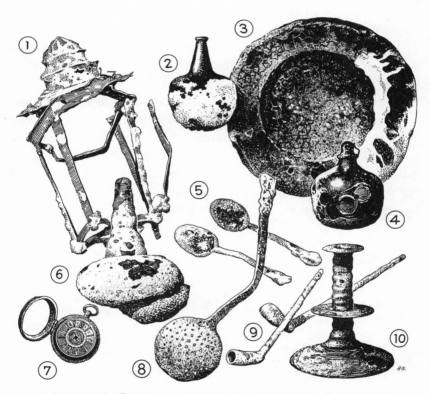

ARTIFACTS FROM PORT ROYAL

1-COPPER LANTERN
2-WINE BOTTLE
3-PEWTER PLATE
4-ONION BOTTLE
5-PEWTER SPOONS

6-GLASS LINEN SMOOTHER
7-POCKET WATCH
8-BRASS SKIMMER
9-CLAY PIPES
10-BRASS CANDLESTICK

as clean as the day the watch had been swept into the sea. Only the iron hands were missing. Link thought perhaps they had disintegrated against the coral and might still be visible in an x-ray photograph. A Kingstown dentist was glad to make the experiment. When the negatives were examined, there was indeed a faint trace of the hands. They pointed to seventeen minutes before twelve—almost the exact moment of the earthquake!

The maker of the watch, Paul Blondel, whose name was engraved on the inside, was identified by the Science Museum of London. He was a French refugee who had worked in Amsterdam. The last known year in which he made watches was 1686.

Ten weeks is a pitifully brief time in which to conduct such an ambitious excavation. The Link expedition proved that Port Royal has a great deal to offer the underwater archaeologist, but it was only the barest beginning. Nevertheless, the Links' careful, detailed preparations have paved the way for future work. In years to come we can expect to learn much more about this fascinating city under the sea.

11

The Sacred Well of the Ancient Maya

IT IS a long way from the mythical continent of Atlantis to the
Yucatán peninsula of Mexico, but a doughty New Eng-
lander covered the distance in one leap. He was the young
American archaeologist Edward Thompson, and his goal was
the ruined Maya Indian city of Chichén Itzá and its forbidding
Well of Sacrifice.

The primitive land of Yucatán, which juts upward like a
gigantic thumb into the blue waters of the Gulf of Mexico, had
beckoned to him since childhood. He had read of it and
dreamed of it. While a student at the Worcester Polytechnic
Institute he had written of it, linking the legendary civilization
of Atlantis with what was then the little-known civilization of
the ancient Maya. Because of his daring article and extensive
studies his dream came true. The officers of the American Antiquarian Society and the Peabody Museum of Harvard University selected him to make a scientific investigation of the
ruins of the Maya Indians. With explorer's knapsack, camera,
and rifle he set out to meet his destiny. The year was 1894.

The first pale rays of dawn had barely streaked the sky when
Thompson left Mérida, the capital city of Yucatán. Throughout the hot and dusty day he traveled the winding jungle trails
on horseback, accompanied by his Indian guide. Night fell and
a brilliant moon rose over the treetops. To the explorer it
seemed as if the trail had no end. His body ached with weari-
ness and he longed to rest. But his curiosity urged him on. At

length he dozed in the saddle, his head bobbing to the rhythm of the horse's plodding footsteps.

Suddenly the Indian spoke to him and earnestly pointed ahead. Thompson raised his eyes. Looming before him was a massive stone pyramid. He had not expected it to be so huge! He shook his head to make sure he was not dreaming. So this, at last, was Chichén Itzá, the sacred city of the ancient Maya. A thrill so intense that it hurt shot through his body.

By the time he dismounted and unsaddled his horse his guide was curled up and fast asleep. For Thompson sleep was out of the question. He scrambled up the ruined stairway of the great pyramid. The ascent was steep and time and again he groped for a handhold, only to have the loose stones slip from his grasp and go tumbling down into the darkness. His feet started minor landslides. His knees and hands were scratched and bruised when he finally reached a narrow stone ledge eighty feet above the ground. Before him was a temple. An immense forty-foot doorway yawned black and mysterious. Thompson peered within and involuntarily shivered with apprehension. Guiltily he realized that he was a trespasser in the domain of the Mayan gods. All about him, faintly illuminated by moonlight, he could see strange and intricate carvings of the great god Kukul Can, the Feathered Serpent.

Turning around, the archaeologist gazed out over the dead city. Here and there a dozen other pyramids rose white and ghostly above the scrubby jungle. Then Thompson caught his breath as he recognized a broad, raised roadway leading straight from the base of the pyramid to a vast, black pool overgrown with trees. From his readings he knew that he was looking at the Sacred Way, and at its end the Sacred Well.

Morning was still several hours away. Thompson inched his way back down the pyramid and lay down beside his guide. His tired body did not feel the hardness of the ground. Instantly he was asleep, but his dreams were filled with the vivid impressions of the night. He was awakened by the heat and light of a fiery sun. While the Indian guide prepared breakfast Thompson trudged down the Sacred Way for his first look at the sacrificial well. It, too, was much larger than he had imagined. In fact, the natural limestone sinkhole looked like a big circular quarry. It was about two hundred feet in diameter. The sides were nearly vertical. Lying down at the edge Thompson gazed at the black waters sixty feet below. His eyes strained to see what secrets lay hidden beneath the surface, but the well was reluctant to reveal its mysteries. All that he could see was the reflection of his own lean, sun-bronzed body.

In the days that followed, Thompson mapped the large overgrown plazas and explored the crumbling temples of Chichén Itzá. Snakes and lizards, basking in the warmth of the tropical sun, rustled ahead of him through the dry grass. Black vultures wheeled far overhead in the cloudless sky. The drone of cicadas filled the air, and only occasionally was the monotony relieved by the cry of a macaw or parrot. Four hundred years had passed since the Itzá lords had sat upon their great stone jaguar throne. Then they had ruled all of Yucatán and had received tribute from provinces as far away as Mexico City and Guatemala. Religious pilgrims had flocked from all directions to throw precious gifts into the Well of Sacrifice. Now all was desolate and abandoned. The Maya Indians, who lived in small villages nearby, were actual descendants of the lords of Chichén Itzá, but they had no more than a faint recollection of their former glory.

The Sacred Well fascinated Thompson. No day of strenuous field work in the ruins was complete for him without a brief period of rest and contemplation at the small temple shrine overlooking the water. From there he could see the Sacred Way, and rising in grandeur above the treetops the pyramid of Kukul Can. Leaning back against the stone ledge he would close his eyes and the centuries would slip away. . . .

It was the year tun 10 in the cycle Katun 8 Ahau of the Maya calendar. Dawn had not yet touched the city of Chichén

Itzá, but already the townspeople were awake and in an eager state of anticipation. Smoke from the breakfast fires rose hazily through the thatch roofs of the houses, and from within them came the low murmur of voices. The Sacred Way was freshly cleaned and adorned with arches and boughs of greenery in preparation for the ritual to come.

In the distance a drum began to beat slowly and resonantly. The men of Chichén Itzá filed out of their houses and gathered along the Sacred Way leading to the Well of Sacrifice. Among them were many pilgrims who had journeyed to the city from all parts of the peninsula of Yucatán. The women and children waited quietly inside the houses. It was not their privilege to participate in the rain ceremony.

Suddenly there was a trilling of flutes and the tempo of the sacred drums increased. From the great doorway of the temple of Kukul Can emerged a procession of Maya priests. They were brilliantly dressed in feather headdresses and robes. Some wore the skins of jaguars, and some had painted their skins blue, the color of sacrifice. Slowly they descended the long stairway of the pyramid and proceeded along the Sacred Way. The men of Chichén Itzá fell into line behind them.

The flutes and drums ceased as the procession reached the shrine at the edge of the Sacred Well. Then, as dawn streaked the sky, the high priest stepped to the rim and addressed the Rain God, Noh-och Yum Chac.

"Oh great Yum Chac, how have we offended you? The corn in our fields is withering, crying for rain. Give us your water for our crops or famine will descend on us and the dread Lord of Death, Ah Puch, will walk abroad in our land. Accept our gifts, great Yum Chac, and be not angry with your people."

One by one the priests stepped to the edge of the well and threw into it precious offerings of copper, jade, and gold. Behind them came the men of the city, in order of rank, with similar gifts for the Rain God.

A young girl, not yet thirteen, was carried up the stairs of the shrine in a flower-bedecked litter. Her body, too, was painted blue. She trembled with fright as the high priest took her hand and led her into the temple. Unseen by the multitude he instructed her in her duties.

"Yours is a great honor, for you will be the messenger of the Rain God. Go to him with our pleas for rain and a bountiful harvest. If he agrees to answer our prayers he will return you to us. Then we will take you from the Well at noon. If he turns from us with a deaf ear we will never see you again, although we know you will not die."

The child cried out in terror and ran weeping to the far corner of the temple. Once again the high priest spoke to her and this time his voice was gentle.

"Take courage and console yourself. We are not doing you harm nor are we casting you into a bad region nor into hell but into heaven and glory in the manner of our ancestors who were accustomed to do so."

The girl fainted as the high priest lifted her in his arms. He strode with her to the edge of the well and raised his voice once more in prayer.

"Great all-powerful Yum Chac, provide us with what we need and give us water for our sustenance."

A sigh arose from the tense crowd as the priest threw the slight body far out toward the center of the well. The shock of the sixty-foot fall and the cold water revived the girl and she struggled instinctively for life. She knew her only chance for survival was to stay afloat until the hour of noon, the time when the procession would return for the message of the Rain God.

Thompson opened his eyes and the vision disappeared. He knew that there had been such ceremonies at the well. They had been described back in 1566 by Diego de Landa, the first Bishop of Yucatán, who came to America on the heels of the Spanish conquerors. For nearly three hundred years after Landa's death his manuscript lay hidden in Madrid. It was a lucky chance that it was not lost. When it was discovered and published it became one of the most important guides to Maya antiquity. Thompson had read it years before making his first visit to Chichén Itzá. One section in particular held his attention:

> From the court in front of these theaters [at Chichén Itzá] runs a wide and handsome roadway as far as the Well, which is about two stones throws off.
>
> Into this Well they have had and still have the custom of throwing men alive as a sacrifice to their gods in time of drought, and they believed they would not die, though they

never saw them again. They also threw into it many other things like precious stones and things they prized, and so if this country had possessed gold it would be this Well that would have the greater part of it, so great is the devotion that the Indians show for it.

Thompson was convinced that a great treasure lay at the bottom of the Sacred Well. He was determined to find a way to recover it.

Eager as Thompson was to probe the mysteries of the Well of Sacrifice he had first to complete his assignment for the American Antiquarian Society and the Peabody Museum. The years passed and it was not until 1909 that he finally began work on his cherished project. In the meantime he purchased the huge hacienda (plantation) of Chichén, and became not only a rancher and planter but the sole owner of the ruined city.

Thompson considered the problem from every possible angle. For days he took measurements and made soundings. Only then did he decide on a course of action. He would need a dredge. He would also have to learn to dive. Thompson set off for the United States to get the equipment, training, and money necessary for the excavation.

When Thompson described his plans to his conservative New England friends they reacted with shocked surprise. Many simply refused to believe the story of the Sacred Well. They were appalled at his plan to dive to the bottom and risk his life in the unknown waters. One friend asked him bluntly: "If you want to commit suicide why not seek a less shocking way of doing it?"

Not in the least daunted, Thompson went to Boston to take lessons in deep-sea diving. While there he adapted to his purpose a special dredge with a stiff-legged derrick, a winch, tackles, steel cables, and a thirty-foot swinging boom. The material was crated and held ready for shipment.

When completely prepared for his daring venture Thompson

made an appointment with the officers of the American Antiquarian Society and the Peabody Museum. They listened with
interest to his plans and were impressed with his careful preparations. At length they agreed to give him the necessary financial aid, but they made it clear that they would accept no
responsibility for his life. Gleefully Thompson ordered the shipment of the dredge.

Back in Yucatán Thompson established what he called a
"fertile zone" in the well by throwing in logs the size and
weight of human bodies. He hoped by so doing to determine
the general area in which the sacrificial victims would have
fallen, and therefore the area where offerings might most likely
be recovered.

At last the day came when the dredge was assembled and
ready for operation. Four men were stationed at the winch
handles and one at the brake. The thirty-foot boom swung out
from the platform, and the dredge with steel jaws agape hung
poised for a brief moment before gliding swiftly downward
through the still, dark waters. There were a few moments of
waiting for the sharp teeth to bite into the bottom. Then the
workmen heaved at the winch handles. Firm muscles tightened
under dark skins as the load was hauled to the surface. The
water surged and boiled and the jaws emerged. A heap of dark
brown material was deposited on the bank and the jaws swung
back for another load.

Thompson leaped to the pile of muck and raked through it,
his heart pounding with excitement. There was nothing but
wood punk, dead leaves, broken branches, and chunks of rock.
The next load was the same as the first. The third and the
fourth were equally disappointing. Evening came and the
workmen left the dredge to return to their homes. Thompson
stared moodily at the murky waters. Then he quietly turned
and walked back along the Sacred Way to his own home.

The days that followed were a repetition of the first. Thompson was nervous by day and sleepless by night. Where were the

offerings? Was the story really nothing but an old-wives' tale? Had he wasted the money of two respected institutions and exposed himself to a world of ridicule? These questions pursued him until he lost his appetite and became thin and haggard from worry.

Week followed barren week. The rainy season began. Thunder rumbled across the sky and streaks of lightning seared the gray clouds. Rain pelted down on the men at the dredge, but the work continued. The pile of muck and rock at the edge of the well grew higher and higher.

One morning Thompson arose after a night of fitful sleep and plodded through the misty, sodden jungle to the well. Even at a distance he could hear the staccato clicks of the dredge brake. Crouching under a palm-leaf lean-to he watched the monotonous motions of the natives as they worked at the winches. The bucket slowly emerged from the water. Thompson walked over and looked listlessly down into it. In the muck were two yellowish-white objects. With a cry of surprise he picked them up and examined them closely. They were made of a resinous substance. Thompson tasted one. Then, trembling with excitement, he threw a piece into a fire. Immediately a wonderful fragrance filled the air. The archaeologist smiled and sat down, weak with relief. He had found two balls of *pom,* the sacred incense of the ancient Mayas and a common offering to the gods. That night for the first time in weeks Thompson ate a hearty meal and slept soundly.

The balls of incense were only the beginning. After that there was scarcely a day when the dredge failed to bring up objects of beauty and scientific interest. Tenderly Thompson cleaned and preserved them. He watched with understandable pride while the collection grew. There were bowls, vases, incense burners, arrowheads, lance points, axes, and hammerstones. The dredge brought up copper chisels; discs of beaten copper; bells, discs, and figures of gold; and beads, pendants, and earrings of green jade. It also brought up the pitiful skeletons of the many men, women, and children who had given their lives to Noh-och Yum Chac, the Rain God.

But finally there came a day when the dredge retrieved nothing but slivers of the rock bottom. Then Thompson knew that the rest of the excavation would have to be done by hand. The time had come for him to go down himself. He sent a wire to his friend Nicolas, a Greek diver who was gathering sponges in the Bahamas. Nicolas left his ship and hurried to Yucatán, bringing with him his assistant.

An air pump was rigged on a pontoon floating on the surface of the well. The two Greeks taught a chosen group of natives how to manage the pumps and send a steady current of air through the tubes. They also taught them to read and answer the signals sent up from below.

The jaws of the dredge were used for transporting men and equipment from the edge of the well to the surface of the water. When all was in readiness Thompson and Nicolas joined the group of natives on the pontoon. The assistant took his place by the men at the pump, while the two divers pulled on their suits. They were clumsy outfits of waterproof canvas with heavy lead necklaces. The canvas shoes had thick wrought-iron soles. Each helped the other to put on his copper helmet, which weighed more than thirty pounds.

Thompson adjusted his speaking tube, air hose, and life line. Then, aided by the assistant, he clumped over to the side of the pontoon where there was a short, wide ladder. As he stepped on the first rung each member of the pumping gang came over to shake his hand. Their solemn faces gave Thompson a bit of a shock. He realized that his good friends were bidding him farewell. The superstitious Indians were sure that they would never see him again. He released his hold on the ladder and sank like a bag of lead to the bottom, seventy feet below.

In his autobiography *The People of the Serpent* Thompson wrote a description of this memorable dive.

During the first ten feet of descent, the light rays changed from yellow to green and then to a purplish black. After that I was in utter darkness. Sharp pains shot through my ears, because of the increasing air pressure. When I gulped and opened the air valves in my helmet a sound like "pht! pht!" came from each ear and then the pain ceased. Several times this process had to be repeated before I stood on the bottom. I noted another curious sensation on my way down. I felt as if I were rapidly losing weight until, as I stood on the flat end of a big stone column that had fallen from the old ruined shrine above, I seemed to have almost no weight at all. I fancied that I was more like a bubble than a man clogged by heavy weights.

But I felt as well a strange thrill when I realized that I was the only living being who had ever reached this place alive and expected to leave it again still living. Then the Greek diver came down beside me and we shook hands.

Although Thompson had gone down prepared with a submarine flashlight and telephone he found that neither of them was very useful. The combination of water and mud in which the two divers worked was much too thick to penetrate with the light. Instead they found that with a little practice their fingertips became so sensitive that they could use them to locate and identify artifacts. They also discovered that if they sat down and put their face plates together they could talk to each other without difficulty.

One day during the excavation a native holy man had pointed to a certain section of the well and said to Thompson: "That is where the Palace of the Rain God lies, as our fathers told us." Thompson dived to the spot indicated and found a deep, natural depression. Around the edge were the outstretched skeletons of three women. One of them wore a necklace of jade beads. Even more remarkable, portions of her dress were still intact. Thompson picked up the fragile pieces and put them in his pouch. While the Greek diver collected the remains of the three skeletons and the jade necklace Thompson signaled that he wished to ascend and was hauled to the surface.

The fragments of cloth were immediately dipped into a preservative and shipped to the Peabody Museum. They are today the only examples of Maya cloth in existence. Each time Thompson and Nicolas entered the well the Indians firmly expected them to be killed by the huge snakes and water monsters believed to live at the bottom. Thompson was too good a naturalist to pay much attention to these stories. Nevertheless they stuck in the back of his mind along with a vague uneasiness each time he descended into the black waters. One day, while busily exploring a narrow crevice of the well floor, an enormous object glided against him and pushed him into the mud. He reached up a hand and felt something smooth and slimy. His blood ran cold. Then Nicolas pushed the object away and they discovered it was nothing but a decayed tree trunk that had drifted down from the mudbank above.

Another incident was far more serious. On one occasion, after finding a remarkable little molded metal bell, the archaeologist became so excited that he forgot to open the air valves of his diving suit. Rising to change position he suddenly found himself soaring to the surface. A moment of shocked surprise was followed immediately by the realization of what had happened. Fumbling desperately with the stopcocks Thompson managed to get the valves opened, but not before he felt explosive pains in both his ears. His quick thinking saved him from what could have been a fatal attack of the bends.

Once the valves were opened Thompson rose more slowly, but he could neither stop his ascent nor control its direction. With a crash he struck the underside of the pontoon and remained there half-dazed by the concussion. The Indians at the pump, hearing the unexpected thump on the bottom of the boat, turned pale with terror. "It's no use," wailed one. "The master is dead. He was swallowed by the Serpent God and

spewed up again. We shall never hear him speak to us again!"
At that moment Thompson's helmet appeared beside the gunwale. The old Indian ran to the side and peered into the face
plate. Raising both arms high above his head he shouted,
"Thank God he is still alive, and laughing!"

As a result of this accident Thompson suffered impaired
hearing for the rest of his life. He considered it a minor penalty
for the privilege of having found the treasure of the Sacred Well.

One of the most interesting side products of Thompson's
underwater excavation of the Sacred Well was the solution of
its oldest mystery. He had often wondered why, of the many
natural wells in Yucatán, this one in particular was believed to
be the home of the Rain God. The other well at Chichén Itzá,
while equally large, had no such reputation. Why, he asked
himself, did those who survived the ordeal of sacrifice swear
that they had seen the gods and heard their voices?

The explanation came to Thompson quite by accident. He
was sitting on the pontoon when he heard voices that seemed to
come from within the well. Peering down into the water he
saw, as if at a great depth, the disembodied heads of several
Maya Indians. The heads conversed softly with each other.
Their words reached him as a low, unintelligible murmur. The
startled archaeologist blinked his eyes and looked again. The
heads continued to talk. Then it dawned on Thompson that
the figures were actually reflections of his own workmen, leaning over the brink of the well to catch a glimpse of the pontoon.
The sound of their voices, as it struck the surface of the water,
was deflected upward to his ears. The effect was unique, possible only because of the steep overhanging walls of the Sacred
Well. Thompson knew at once that he had discovered the key
to the old tradition.

In his autobiography he commented: "I have come to believe that all authentic traditions have a basis of fact and can
always be explained by a sufficiently close observation of the
conditions."

When the excavation was completed Thompson packed the treasure and sent it to the Peabody Museum of Harvard. Since the Museum had paid for the project it seemed only logical that all the material should go to them. Some years later the Mexican government decided otherwise. Demanding the return of the treasure, they confiscated Thompson's Yucatán plantation and forced him to return to the United States. Lawyers went to work on both sides. After many years and innumerable lawsuits the Mexican courts decreed that Thompson had acted legally. At the time he had sent the relics to the Peabody Museum there were no laws forbidding their exportation. Nevertheless the incident remained a source of friction between Mexico and the United States.

Good will was finally restored in 1960 when Harvard University returned ninety-four of the priceless Maya ornaments to Mexico. They now gleam with special splendor in the National Archaeological Museum of Mexico City. Thompson, were he still alive, would doubtlessly be pleased at the harmonious conclusion of a long and bitter quarrel.

There are many other natural wells in Yucatán. The entire peninsula is made up of a porous limestone that is honeycombed with subterranean streams, channels, and caves. When the surface caved in, a natural well or *cenote* was formed. In the dry season these wells still provide the only water supply, since there are no lakes or surface streams in Yucatán. The Mayan cities grew up around them and life was dependent upon them. It is little wonder that certain wells came to be considered the sacred home of the Rain God.

In spite of Thompson's spectacular discoveries no further investigations were made in Yucatán for almost half a century. Then in 1956 two divers from the University of Florida, David Conklin and Whitney Robinet, began underwater investigations of a *cenote* at Dzibilchaltun. This ruined Maya city is located seventy-five miles from Chichén Itzá, and although

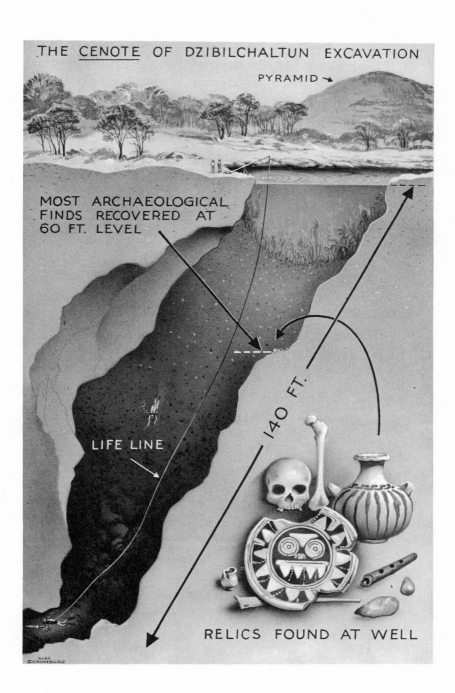

THE <u>CENOTE</u> OF DZIBILCHALTUN EXCAVATION

PYRAMID →

MOST ARCHAEOLOGICAL FINDS RECOVERED AT 60 FT. LEVEL

140 FT.

LIFE LINE

RELICS FOUND AT WELL

ALEX
SCHOMBURG

smaller it is somewhat older. There are more than a dozen wells at the site, but the one that seemed most promising was located in the very center of the ruins. It was also the largest.

The following year the project was taken over by the National Geographic Society. It sent down its ace diver-photographer, Luis Marden, and a diver and staff photographer by the name of Bates Littlehales. The archaeological project was supervised by Dr. E. Wyllys Andrews of the Middle American Research Institute of Tulane University in New Orleans. The divers used Aqualungs and worked from a diving platform located just below the water level of the well. They kept in contact with the surface by a life line.

The well was one hundred feet across at its widest point and a hundred and forty feet deep. Most of the material, however, was recovered on the sloping walls about sixty feet down. Broken earthenware pots lay thick among the rubble of carved stone that had fallen from the pyramid at the well's edge. Among the special finds were an engraved bone awl with a vertical row of hieroglyphs, a clay flute, a figurine head, numerous obsidian knives, bone noseplugs, and a few human bones. Many of these items were probably offerings to the Rain God, although some could have fallen into the well by accident when their owners came for water.

While the *cenote* of Dzibilchaltun was being explored other divers far to the south in the country of Guatemala were finding even more spectacular gifts to the Maya Rain God.

12

Gifts to the Rain God

IT was the kind of night feared by primitive people all over the world, and the Maya Indians of highland Guatemala were no exception. Brave men pulled the blankets tight around their shoulders and children shivered in their mothers' arms, as the heavens roared their fury. Thunder crackled and boomed from mountain peak to mountain peak. Torrents of rain roiled the surface of Lake Amatitlán, and in the neighboring village of San Juan Amatitlán newborn rivulets swirled about the mud and thatch houses and cascaded over the cobbled streets. The earth heaved and shuddered. The fourth and newest cone of the volcano Pacaya glowed red in the black night. Behind the massive stone walls of the church of San Juan Amatitlán a little group of Dominican friars knelt in prayer. The flames of their candles flickered with each gust of wind that sighed down the long corridors of the cloister.

Dawn came at last and brought the welcome sun to warm the earth and reassure its people that the terror of the night was past. The first rays had barely touched the hills when the Indian farmers of Amatitlán ate their breakfast of coffee and tortillas and hurried to the cornfields to repair the damage of the storm.

Some farmers stopped, as was their custom, to pay their respects to the stone idol, Jefe Diós or Chief God. No one knew how long he had stood on the edge of the cliff overlooking Lake Amatitlán. The old people said he had been there since the beginning of time, but since the arrival of the Spaniards Jefe Diós had been worshiped in secret.

The Indians of Amatilán were not pagans. They had listened intently to the teachings of the Spanish priests and in due time they had been baptized as Christians. But their loyalty and fear of the old Maya god were too strong to be forgotten. For years they had avoided the watchful eyes of the Dominican friars and stolen away to visit the hiding place of Jefe Diós. Surely, they reasoned, the Christian God would not be jealous if they burned a few candles and some incense and made a few sacrificial offerings of fruits and animals to their old friend and protector.

On the morning after the storm the first man to make the climb up the steep cliff to the pagan shrine was Juan Yax. He pushed aside the covering of wet branches and called to his companions: "Santiago, Pedro, come quickly! Something terrible has happened! Jefe Diós is gone!"

The two friends scrambled up the path to the shrine. Before them were the blunt ends of candles burned the night before. The ground was strewn with marigolds, the sacred flower, but Jefe Diós was nowhere to be seen.

"Was the storm so violent that he fell over the cliff?" asked Santiago.

The three men crawled to the edge and looked down. Far below them the blue waters of the lake glittered in the sun. There was no sign of Jefe Diós, but something strange caught their eye. On a projection of rock a few feet above the water's edge they saw a small, painted wooden figure. The Indians looked at each other with solemn eyes.

"It is a figure of the Christ Child!" whispered Juan.

"The Christ Child has overthrown the old god," gasped Pedro.

The men reverently made the sign of the cross and hurried off to spread word of the miracle.

As soon as the Dominican friars heard the news they declared a day of festival and rejoicing. A procession of boats and canoes was organized, and the townspeople and the priests crossed the lake to the spot where the figure of the Christ Child had so suddenly appeared. The statue was brought to the church on the plaza and placed with great ceremony on a special altar. News of the miraculous image spread far and wide, and Indians came from every part of Guatemala to be cured of their ills and to ask that their prayers be granted.

All this happened in the early seventeenth century or so the legend goes. There are skeptics who wonder if one of the good friars may not have personally performed God's work by throwing old Jefe Diós into the lake and installing the Christ Child in his place. There are no skeptics, however, among the simple Maya Indians. To them the disappearance of the stone idol and the appearance of the Christian image was, and has remained, a true miracle. It is commemorated yearly on May 3rd, the Day of the Holy Cross.

On this day devout pilgrims gather in Amatitlán. At dawn firecrackers awake the sleeping townspeople and announce the beginning of the fiesta. Soon the plaza in front of the gaily-decorated church is full of eager celebrants. Merchants sell religious candles and the famous Amatitlán candies from makeshift stalls set up for the occasion. The bells of the church clang out a noisy welcome and invite the visitors to hear Mass. Before the church door sits a drummer. He is accompanied by another man playing a *chirimia,* the native Mayan flute. The music they play is very old. It has not changed for untold generations. To our ears it seems strange, repetitious, and almost tuneless.

At the appointed hour the carved wooden doors of the church open. A procession of priests, carrying the figure of the Christ Child, emerges. The crowd falls in line behind the priests and follows them to the main pier on the lake. A special boat has been prepared to carry the statue across the lake to the spot where it first appeared. The boat is festooned with crêpe paper ribbons and has a huge red cross mounted on the front. The fishing boats have been decorated in a similar fashion. Everyone who can crowd into a boat does so. Those who cannot, wade out into the water to see the others off. The local military band strikes up a stirring march. The people wave gaily to their friends on shore and prepare to throw their offerings of fruit and flowers into the lake in honor of the Christ Child.

Anthropologists had considered the fiesta of Amatitlán to be colorful and interesting. They might never have known of its pre-Christian origins were it not for a group of enthusiastic skin divers, who began using their Aqualungs to explore the lake for good fishing grounds. The "fish" they found started a most interesting underwater investigation.

Lake Amatitlán is a beautiful resort area seventeen miles south of Guatemala City. Although it is in the tropics its location in a mountain valley four thousand feet above sea level gives it a climate that is never cold and rarely too hot. Rising majestically from the south shore of the lake is the active four-coned volcano Pacaya. Seething fires deep within the earth are responsible for innumerable hot-water springs and occasionally a geyser. In certain areas the sulphurous water that bubbles from the lake bottom or along the shore is hot enough to boil an egg.

The Indians make great use of the warm water for bathing and for washing clothes, but its importance to them goes far beyond mere convenience. They believe the waters are possessed of magical curative properties. In Spanish colonial times the area was famous as a health resort, until an epidemic of malaria wiped out most of the population. Today, with malaria firmly under control, Indians come from great distances to bathe in the healing waters, and two lakeside hotels offer thermal baths to wealthier visitors. The lower end of the lake is lined with weekend cottages, and in good weather it is the scene of water sports of all kinds.

In 1954 a group of young Guatemalans decided to introduce
the sport of Aqualung diving to Lake Amatitlán. A year later
one of the group, Manfred Töpke, made a surprising discovery.
While swimming along the lake bottom he touched a hard,
circular object buried in the soft mud. The water was too
murky to see what it was, but out of curiosity he decided to dig
it up. To his amazement he found a large clay incense burner
richly adorned with sculptured designs. Töpke recognized it as
an archaeological specimen of considerable importance. He
notified his friends and they began looking for similar relics.
Within two years divers had amassed collections amounting
to more than six hundred pottery vessels, incense burners, and
stone sculptures. The supply of pottery in the lake seemed inexhaustible. The divers decided it was time an archaeologist was
called in to examine their material. In 1957 Dr. Stephan F. de
Borhegyi, a Hungarian-born American archaeologist, was in
Guatemala teaching classes at San Carlos University. He was
asked to look at the specimens, which the divers modestly told
him were "a collection of old pots from the lake." One glance
convinced him that the material constituted one of the great
Mayan discoveries of the century. He set to work immediately
to plan a thorough underwater investigation of Lake Amatitlán.

His first step was to catalog, classify, and photograph the
material already recovered. Fortunately the divers had made
their collections with considerable care. They had carried
depth gauges and taken accurate notes, numbering the specimens according to their original location. De Borhegyi found
that most of the material had come from nine underwater deposits, seven of them near hot springs off the south shore, the
other two in deeper water off the north shore. The specimens
ranged from a few inches to four and one-half feet in height.
The incense burners bore unusual designs: cacao trees and
pods, papaya fruits and flowers, quetzal birds, hummingbirds,
jaguar heads, spider monkeys, snakes, lizards, bats, and even
human skulls. Many of them were decorated with sculptured

human heads peering from the jaws or beaks of animals, monsters, and birds. Among the Mayan gods depicted were the Rain God, Yum Chac or Tlaloc; the Jaguar God; the Sun God; the Wind God, Eecatl; a Fertility God, Xipe Totec; and the Death God. The magnificently-sculptured vessels were clearly offerings of a very special kind. Like those found in the Sacred Well of Chichén Itzá, they were dedicated during rain ceremonies to the powerful Mayan Rain God.

Since certain types of vessels and designs seemed to be restricted to particular underwater localities De Borhegyi began to suspect that each underwater deposit represented a different time period. To confirm the time sequence he decided to make a thorough investigation of all archaeological sites on land in the vicinity of the lake. Several of these had been discovered and mapped earlier by members of the Guatemalan research team of the Carnegie Institution of Washington. They were re-studied, and three new sites were discovered by De Borhegyi and his research team of students from San Carlos University. Meanwhile De Borhegyi asked his crew of divers to make a list of observations and measurements on the underwater sites.

The next step was a check of all reports and documents, scientific and historical, that dealt with the Amatitlán area. The geology of the region; the plants, fish, and wildlife; the lake waters; and the customs and traditions of the modern inhabitants were analyzed. One early historical document that proved very useful was the *Account Book of the Town of San Juan Amatitlán,* written during the years 1559–1562 and now in the archives of the Smithsonian Institution of Washington. The historian, Fuentes y Guzmán, writing in 1690, mentioned the town briefly and included a crude map of the lake area showing a group of ruins on the south shore, which he called Tzacualpa. By far the most interesting information on the Spanish colonial period was supplied by the writings of an enterprising English Dominican friar, Thomas Gage, who had been parish priest of San Juan Amatitlán during the year 1635–1636.

MAYAN PRIEST MAKES OFFERING TO THE RAIN GOD

Other scientists were asked to examine the material. Botanists identified the stylized plant designs and described the kind of climate in which the plants would have grown. Zoologists identified the bird and animal figures. Geologists studied samples of volcanic rock taken from the lake bottom and supplied information on the type and date of volcanic eruptions and their effect on the lake and its people.

When all the information was collected De Borhegyi began the job of correlation. He compared the material from the underwater sites with that collected by his crew on land, and whenever possible with similar artifacts found in other parts of the Mayan area. The result was a continuous record of almost three thousand years of human history.

The Amatitlán story began to take form about a thousand years before the birth of Christ. The first settlers, like their descendants, were farmers. They ate fish from the lake and hunted game animals, but their steady diet consisted of corn and black beans. Good weather meant a bountiful harvest. A severe drought often meant famine. Of all the many Mayan gods, the Rain God understandably came to be the most respected. The very livelihood of the Mayan farmers depended upon his blessing. They associated him with thunder and lightning, and with springs and wells. The presence of awesome hot springs and geysers on the shore of Lake Amatitlán, combined with a fear of the rumbling, rock spewing volcano Pacaya, could easily have convinced them that particularly powerful spirits or gods dwelt in the lake. As early as 500 B.C. the first offerings were cast into the lake waters.

The centuries passed, and the population around the lake flourished. Around 200 A.D. some of the earlier sites were abandoned in favor of new ones. The new cities were larger, and contained many temple mounds to honor the Mayan gods. There were courts for ceremonial ball games and plazas for religious festivities and markets. The hill slopes were carefully terraced for more efficient farming.

One of the sites of this period, built at the water's edge amidst numerous hot springs, consists today of only four small mounds. In all likelihood it was a shrine. Judging from the immense number of specimens found in the nearby underwater deposit the Indians came there in droves, bringing rich and varied offerings. The offerings were so elaborate that they may have been made specifically for the Rain God.

Human sacrifice, or at least offerings of bodies of the dead, was probably not uncommon. One bowl was found containing the upper section of the skull of a young woman. It had been painted with red ocher and was obviously a special offering. Even long after the introduction of Christianity there were occasional rumors of child sacrifices to the lake.

From about 1000 A.D. to the Spanish conquest in 1524 the entire Mayan area was torn by intertribal warfare. The old cities near the lake shore were abandoned in favor of others built in less accessible and more easily-defended locations on the tops of hills. To make their offerings the Indians crossed the lake in canoes to two sites on the north shore. Both sites were near the spot, where according to legend the stone idol Jefe Diós had his shrine, and where the offerings are made today to the figure of the Christ Child. For the Spanish priests, arriving soon after the conquest of Guatemala, did their best to force the Indians away from their old religious beliefs.

In recent years there has been a mild climatic change in the Guatemalan highlands. The rains have been irregular. They have been long delayed and then have come in such violent outbursts that they have caused floods and crop damage. In 1959 there was a series of mild earthquakes. The Indians look knowingly at each other. The old Rain God, they say, is angry at the skin divers, who have desecrated his sacred lake and taken away his offerings. Somewhere down at the bottom of Lake Amatitlán one can almost hear the soft, mocking laughter of Jefe Diós.

13

Spanish Galleons and Sunken Gold

UNTIL the end of the fifteenth century the Mayas were free to live their lives as they saw fit. They and their neighbors, the Aztecs of Mexico and the Incas of Peru, developed great civilizations that were all the more remarkable because they were built on the basis of Stone-Age cultures. Of metals they knew only gold, silver, and copper, and these were too soft to be used for anything but ornamental purposes. All work was done with stone or fire-hardened wooden tools. They had no carts or carriages, for they never made use of the wheel. Except for the balky llama of the Incas they had no beasts of burden. Their only domesticated animals were the dog, the turkey, the llama, and the bee.

Yet they built large and beautiful cities and linked them with a vast network of highways. Their rulers led lives of the greatest luxury. Their priests made exacting astronomical observations and with them created a calendar the equal of our own. They invented systems of hieroglyphic writing and produced many artistically-illustrated books. They worshiped a multitude of gods and built for them lofty and imposing temples. They fought battles and formed empires.

Then one day three small sailing ships reached the shores of the New World. . . .

When Christopher Columbus discovered the western hemisphere in 1492 he set in motion one of the most eventful periods in history. The seeds of world conquest and exploration had been sown in Europe years before, but the discovery of a new continent of vast proportions and unheard-of wealth presented a challenge unique in the long history of the world.

Here was opportunity for everyone: adventure for the restless, danger for those who wanted glory, pagans for the missionaries, strange customs for the writers and historians, rich agricultural lands for the farmers, and above all gold and silver for the greedy. The great names march across the pages of history. After Columbus came Cortes, who conquered the Aztecs. Montejo and Alvarado conquered the Mayas. Balboa stood "upon a peak of Darien" and saw for the first time the immensity of the Pacific Ocean. The Pizarro brothers—Francisco, Gonzalo, and Hernando—conquered the Incas of Peru.

The zeal of the Spaniards derived from two rather opposite goals. On the one hand they wanted to "save" the Indians by destroying their pagan gods and converting them to Christianity. On the other they wished to exploit them as slaves. The lands they conquered were incredibly rich in gold, silver, and jade, and the sight of so much wealth drove the Spanish to excesses which we find difficult to excuse today. Many Indians were enslaved and put to work in the mines. They were assigned harsh quotas of gold and silver. Death was the penalty for not meeting the assignment. For a while it really seemed as if the supply of mineral wealth were inexhaustible.

During the three hundred years from 1520 to 1820 the equivalent in United States currency of eight billions in gold and silver was transported across the Atlantic. One-fifth of the proceeds of the mines belonged to the Spanish crown. This was collected and recorded in the *Casa de Contratacion* or House of Trade in Madrid.

The treasures arrived in Spain twice yearly, transported in great fleets. One fleet, named the *Galleones,* brought the treasure of the Incas from the Andes, gold from Venezuela and Peru, silver from Potosí in Bolivia, and pearls and emeralds from Margarita, Venezuela, and Guayaquil in Ecuador. The other fleet, named the *Flota,* carried the Aztec hoard, silver from the mines of Zacatecas and gold from Tehuantepec. The two fleets met in Havana, Cuba, where they were joined by Spanish men-of-war for protection on the long voyage home. Leaving the port of Havana, they sailed in a northeasterly direction to the Straits of Florida. Then altering their course to the northward they cruised along the Gulf stream until at last they reached the open sea. This passage may have been the best exit from the "Indies," but in bad weather it became a death trap.

The Caribbean is well known as the mother of hurricanes. The Spanish galleons were handsome and imposing, but they were built more for good looks than for efficiency. They were tall and square, and plunged and tossed in a heavy sea. Even in calm weather a miscalculation on the part of the navigator sometimes sent one crashing into reefs and shoals hidden just below the surface of the water. They were preyed upon by British, French, and Dutch ships, and by pirates who owed allegiance only to themselves. Pirates found the Florida Keys and the Bahamas ideally suited to their trade. There were innumerable bays and inlets, where they could lie in wait for their victims or hide when pursued. Often they were aided by the sudden storms characteristic of the Caribbean and the Gulf of Mexico. They pounced eagerly on wrecked and helpless ships, and then scurried away in the fog before they could be caught. However, the enemy ships that preyed upon the Spanish treasure fleets often became victims of other marauders or were themselves wrecked. Today, beneath the sands and coral of the Mexican coast, the Bahamas, and the Florida Keys, lie the remains of hundreds of sixteenth-, seventeenth-, and eighteenth-century ships. For years they have presented an irresistible challenge to treasure hunters. Now they are just as irresistible to the underwater archaeologist and historian.

Probably the most rewarding treasure hunt of all time took

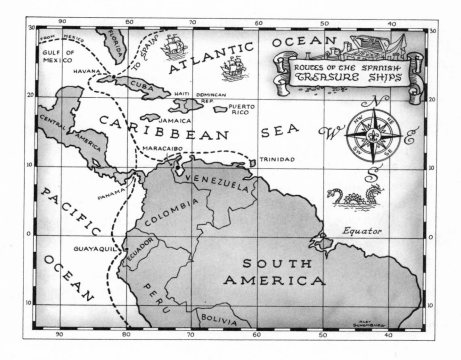

place in the year 1687, when a ship's carpenter from Bristol, Maine, recovered 1,490,000 English pounds in gold and silver from a sunken Spanish galleon. His name was William Phips.

Phips first heard of the wrecked galleon and its vast cargo of Spanish treasure in 1681. He carefully tracked down all the information available, including a chart of the approximate position of the wreck on what was then known as the Ambrosian reef in the Bahamas. Then, since he was almost penniless, he sailed for England to get money for his treasure hunt. Phips's scheme soon reached the ears of the second Duke of Albemarle, a titled but equally penniless nobleman who dreamed of acquiring an easy fortune. Albemarle introduced Phips to the King of England, Charles II, who was so impressed by the treasure tale that he made Phips the captain of a frigate named the *Algier Rose* and sent him off to the Bahamas with his bless-ing.

In the Bahamas Phips was beset with troubles. Months were spent scanning the reefs and shoals without finding a sign of the promised wreck. Eventually his crew of ninety-five sailors grew restless and decided to turn to piracy. Phips avoided the mutiny by heading for Port Royal, where he tricked most of the men into going ashore. While they were gone he signed on a new crew and hurriedly set sail. More months passed in a fu-tile search for the wreck. Provisions were running low, Phips had no money to buy more, and the *Algier Rose* was leaking badly. Two years after he started out a dejected Phips returned to England, only to find that Charles II had died and a new king, James II, sat on the throne.

The Duke of Albemarle was still enthusiastic, but he could not persuade King James to furnish royal funds for a second expedition. He therefore organized a syndicate called the "Gentlemen Adventurers" to furnish the ships, wages, and sup-plies. In return the Duke promised each member one-eighth of the treasure. According to royal law the King was still entitled to a tenth. The Duke demanded one-fourth for his efforts, but Phips was to receive only one-sixteenth of a share, because he was not a "gentleman."

In September, 1686, Phips headed again for the Bahamas, this time in command of a two hundred-ton frigate, the *James and Mary,* followed by the smaller fifty-ton *Henry of London.* His luck was spectacular. The wreck was discovered almost imme-diately, wedged upright on a reef in only forty-five feet of wa-ter. In the three months from January to April Phips and his men worked feverishly. In spite of terrible weather that con-stantly threatened the ships with destruction on the treacher-ous reefs four English divers and several native Bahamians made hundreds of descents. They hoisted up tons of silver in coined dollars and pigs of metal, silver dishes, jars, and plates.

Phips was in such fear of pirates that he dared not linger. In

April he set out for England, and on June 6, 1687, sailed triumphantly up the Thames river. Not only did Phips receive his promised share of the treasure, but he was knighted by the King and made the Royal Governor of Massachusetts.

Ever since, the reefs and cays of the Gulf of Mexico and the Caribbean have been the challenge and the despair of treasure hunters. Since few successful treasure hunts are publicized because of the inevitable problem of ownership and taxation there is no way of knowing how much wealth has been recovered. Unquestionably there is still Spanish gold and silver at the bottom of the sea. The promoters of treasure hunts make it sound so tempting. Why hasn't it been found?

When a ship hit a reef it seldom sank on the spot. It usually bounced along in the boiling surf, tearing great holes in its hull and spilling its contents along the way. The gold and silver, which was often hidden under the ballast in the bilges, was strewn amid the sand and rocks. Any large objects, such as cannon, were raised whenever possible. Whatever was left was then picked clean by the Calusa Indians of the Florida Keys who were excellent skin divers.

The wooden ship was often burned to keep it from being salvaged by enemy hands. Any remaining wood was soon demolished by shipworms. Porcelain and earthenware objects were disguised by calcareous sea growths. In a few years iron objects were covered by a natural coral cement, formed from the corrosion products of iron combined with coral sand. Even cannon and anchors that could not be salvaged soon assumed the exact color and texture of their surroundings. To be successful a treasure hunter had to know exactly where to look, what to look for, and how to recognize it despite its natural camouflage. He also had to contend with the storms and bad weather that are synonymous with the Caribbean, and which make surface visibility impossible and navigation hazardous.

With the invention of skin-diving equipment treasure hunting assumed tremendous, but not surprising, popularity. During the 1950's the waters of the Florida straits and the Bahamas were explored by thousands of divers, all in the hopes of finding something like Phips's treasure trove. A few found bars of silver; most returned with cannon balls, anchors, and such assorted bits as buttons, coins, and ships' fittings. It was obvious that the material, though of little monetary value, was of considerable historical importance. One of the first to recognize this was a veteran diver and underwater photographer by the name of Arthur McKee, Jr.

With so much historical material being discovered it was also obvious that a professional historian was needed to direct the treasure hunting. Ed Link, whom we have already met as the leader of the Port Royal expedition, made this possible. With his financial support the Smithsonian Institution in Washington organized the Marine Archaeology Project. Link offered to perform a major part of the exploratory work from his converted and especially-equipped shrimp boat, the *Sea Diver*. This craft was the predecessor of the one used in the Port Royal excavation. Mendel L. Peterson, Curator of the Division of Naval History of the United States National Museum, was chosen to direct the project. He was ideally suited for the job. Not only was he a trained historian, he was also a skilled diver.

The wrecked ships from two famous maritime disasters have been favorite targets for treasure hunters over the years. There were fifteen ships in the fleet that sailed from Havana, Cuba, on Friday, the 13th of July, 1733, under the command of Don Rodrigo de Torres. Not only the day was unlucky. It was the hurricane season and a bad time of year for ships to leave the Indies. The merchant ships, heavily loaded with rich cargos of silver, cochineal dye, and mahogony were led by the galleon, *Rubí*, and squired by three two-decker warships. They had just entered the Florida straits when the wind began to blow from the north with gale force. The strong norther continued until noon the next day. Then, suddenly, the wind shifted and moved to all points of the compass before finally blowing from the southeast. Since the fleet could find no secure anchorage in the mile-deep waters of the Gulf stream, it was at the mercy of the storm. De Torres ordered each ship to make its way to the east, and the fleet split up. Several of the galleons were driven over the reefs of the Florida Keys and sank; others were blown onto the beaches. Before the hurricane moved on, eight of the gallant vessels had been lost.

One ship, believed to be the galleon *El Capitan,* was discovered by Arthur McKee off Fisherman's Tip, east of Plantation Key, Florida, in 1949. In May, 1953, the Smithsonian Marine Archaeological Project joined the treasure hunt. Diving among the coral shoals McKee, Link, and Peterson found cannon, iron ship fittings, pewter bowls, a four-and-a-half inch solid silver idol—probably an Aztec goddess of fertility—and a six-foot silver figure of a Spanish dancing girl. A coin minted in Mexico City was found bearing the date 1731. Link checked with coin collectors and found that it was very rare. Almost the entire issue went to the bottom of the sea with De Torres' fleet.

The booty retrieved during a treasure hunt rarely equals the cost of the expedition. There is no better example than the many divers who have spent fortunes in search of the treasure galleons of Vigo Bay on the west coast of Spain.

In the year 1702 a group of British and Dutch warships combined forces to attack a large fleet of seventeen French and Spanish galleons, loaded with gold and silver from the Indies. The galleons had taken refuge in the bay only to find that they were securely bottled up by the enemy warships. There was a terrible naval battle. The defenders fought bravely, but when defeat seemed certain the commander of the fleet issued an order to scuttle the treasure ships. His plan to put the precious cargo beyond the reach of his enemies did not entirely succeed. The British and Dutch sailors fought furiously to salvage the gold and silver from the sinking ships, and a considerable

THE BATTLE AT VIGO BAY

amount was transferred to two British warships. To compound
the tragedy one of them, the *Monmouth,* hit a hidden rock as it
moved out of Vigo Bay. It sank immediately, and the millions
in gold and silver went to the bottom.

Through the years there have been more than seventy unsuccessful expeditions to salvage the treasure from the *Monmouth* and from the French and Spanish galleons lost in Vigo
Bay. As recently as 1955 a group of American divers obtained
a salvage concession from the Spanish government at a cost of
five thousand dollars. They had gathered such detailed records
of the battle and the sinkings that they felt assured of success.
Locating the wrecks turned out to be an easy matter. However,
all that remained of the *Monmouth* was deck rubble, cannon
balls, chain, and lead sheathing. There was no sign of the
treasure. The French and Spanish galleons were buried under
tons of silt. Even though from ten to thirty feet of mud was removed by a hydraulic pump from each wreck, and every bit of
this mud sifted with infinite care, not one precious item was
found. After a year of vigorous but unrewarded searching the
venture ended in failure. What became of the treasure? It may
still lie hidden at the bottom of the bay, or it may have been salvaged bit by bit over the years by the Spanish fishermen who
live in the region. The historical material recovered by the divers helped considerably to make up for the lack of gold and
silver.

The most spectacular treasure found in recent years, both
because of its historical and its monetary value, was recovered
in 1955 by Edward B. (Teddy) Tucker. Since the age of twelve,
Tucker, a native of Bermuda, had fished and dived and explored the jagged reefs and coves of his island. In the course
of his wanderings he found so many wrecks that he decided
to go into the treasure-hunting business.

It was on a pleasant Sunday afternoon in 1955 that Tucker
and his brother-in-law, Robert Canton, decided to investigate
at close quarters a wreck they had spotted some five years

earlier. Digging around in the sand with their hands in the shallow water of an off-shore reef they found a bronze apothecary's mortar marked Petrus Van Den Ghein and dated 1561. Really excited, the two dived down again and this time uncovered a pile of silver coins, all black with silver sulphide and stuck together with coral. Next they found a small bar of gold glittering brightly in the sand. In the ten days that followed, more gold bars were dug up, along with nuggets, jewelry, and hundreds of French and Spanish silver coins. By far the most valuable piece was a bishop's gold pectoral cross studded with seven emeralds.

All of this material was studied by Mendel Peterson. Although the ship, which he recognized as a late sixteenth-century Spanish galleon, is still unnamed, he identified the Petrus Van Den Ghein of the apothecary's mortar as a famous Flemish bronze caster who died in 1561. The bishop's cross now hangs in splendor in Tucker's popular Wreck Museum in Hamilton, Bermuda.

14
Along North Atlantic Shores

ENGLAND did not begin to colonize North America until the seventeenth century, although her claim to it was established as early as 1497. Five years after Columbus made his first voyage to the New World one of his countrymen, the Italian navigator Giovanni Caboto, landed on what is now the coast of Canada and took possession of it in the name of Henry VII of England. Caboto, later known as John Cabot, had come to England as early as 1484 to find support for an exploratory expedition. He, too, believed that an all-water route to the Indies lay straight west across the Atlantic Ocean. No one paid much attention to him, however, until news of Columbus' discoveries reached the British Isles. Then King Henry belatedly sent Cabot on his way. It was a decisive moment in English history, but Cabot like Columbus never knew the magnitude of his discovery. He thought he had landed on the northeast coast of Asia.

The British made no immediate effort to follow up Cabot's discovery. During most of the sixteenth century Spanish men-of-war ruled the Atlantic, and the Spanish king, Philip II, grew rich and powerful with the wealth of the New World. Queen Elizabeth I, who ascended the British throne in 1558, turned a jealous eye on her southern neighbor, but knew she was not strong enough to openly challenge Spanish sea power. Instead, she played a waiting game. Quietly and unofficially she commissioned private ships to plunder the Spanish treasure galleons. The privateers, expert and daring seamen, succeeded in diverting a sizeable share of New World gold and silver into the English treasury. King Philip complained bitterly of these outrages to Elizabeth. Indignantly she denied having anything to do with them. How could he suggest, she cried, that the Queen of England would ally herself with buccaneers!

By the time Philip lost patience with the wily Elizabeth she had built the English navy into an aggressive and efficient fighting force. In 1588 the "invincible Spanish Armada," sent to punish England, was soundly trounced by a much smaller fleet of British warships. Spain never really recovered from the blow to its power and prestige. But Britain, the groundwork laid for her eventual mastery of the seas, was ready at last to think seriously of colonization.

Many of the British ships that sailed from England to America were destined for a watery grave along the North Atlantic shores. One of the first of these was an emigrant ship named the *Sea Venture*. Important for its role in British and American colonial history, the ship also had an impact on English literature. Three hundred and fifty years later it made headlines simply by being discovered.

It was in the summer of 1609 that the *Sea Venture* loosened sail and headed across the Atlantic. Its destination was the infant colony of Jamestown, founded two years earlier, and now desperately in need of reinforcements and supplies from England. Much larger than the *Mayflower,* the three hundred-ton *Sea Venture* was the flagship of a fleet of nine vessels. In the hold were a hundred and fifty settlers and a full load of provisions for the starving colonists in Virginia.

The first half of the trip was uneventful, but as the fleet neared the Virginia coast it was beset by a terrible storm and the *Sea Venture* was separated from its companion ships. For days the wind shrieked through the rigging and the ship tossed and leaped like a cork in the heavy seas. Only the efforts of the crew, who bailed water day and night, kept it afloat. In the hold the passengers clung to each other and to the heavy posts that supported the deck. It was a frightful experience and few expected to survive. Admiral George Somers was aware that his ship was being blown far off course, so it was with considerable relief that he finally spotted the island of Bermuda the morning of July 28, 1609. Finding no safe harbor he reluctantly ordered the vessel grounded between two heads of coral. The unfortunate *Sea Venture* stayed afloat only long enough for her passengers to get safely ashore in the ship's longboat and to be stripped of everything usable and portable.

The castaways were delighted with their haven. Since it was uninhabited they promptly laid claim to it in the name of the king of England. The climate was mild and food was abundant. Wild pigs roamed the island in great numbers, descendants of domesticated pigs set ashore years earlier by Spanish explorers. The sea offered a variety of fish and shellfish and there were many wild turtles and pigeons.

Nine months after being shipwrecked the passengers of the *Sea Venture* completed the building of two small vessels and continued their voyage to Virginia. They found the Jamestown colonists on the verge of starvation and besieged by Indians. The food brought from Bermuda saved the lives of the settlers and assured the continuation of the colony. It was a happy ending to what was so nearly a tragedy.

One of the passengers on board the *Sea Venture,* by the name of Silvanus Jourdan, published in 1610 an account of the voyage. It is believed that Shakespeare was so impressed with the exciting sea story that he used it as the basis for what is thought to be his last play, *The Tempest.*

Three-and-a-half centuries later a descendant of one of the *Sea Venture*'s passengers, Edmund Downing of Virginia, became interested in the story. It occurred to him that remains of the emigrant ship must still exist somewhere on the Bermuda coast. Since he was a skilled diver he determined to find them. He began his search by tracking down every reference to the wreck. According to Jourdan the ship "fell in betweene two rocks." A plaque on the island of Bermuda said the ship sank "under a point that bore South East from a Northern point of the island." In the Bermuda archives an old document was found that gave the wreck's distance from shore as three-quarters of a mile.

Downing succeeded in locating the *Sea Venture* on the afternoon of October 18, 1959. At a depth of thirty-five feet he made out the faint outlines of her keel and ribs, etched in the sand between the two heads of coral exactly where the Admiral had grounded her 350 years earlier. The sea floor was covered with pieces of flint, a common ballast in sixteenth- and seventeenth-century ships. Sometime later Teddy Tucker, Bermuda's wreck expert, joined the salvage operations. Together the divers excavated a large cannon, seventy-five to eighty cannon balls, a stone jug, and a pewter spoon. These were sent to the Smithsonian Institution for analysis, and shortly afterward Mendel Peterson was flown to Bermuda for an on-the-spot inspection. After a thorough examination of the wreck he announced that it was, without a doubt, the ill-fated *Sea Venture*. The discovery came just in time to be celebrated along with Bermuda's 350th anniversary.

Another ship to achieve recent recognition for its role in American colonial history lay more than two hundred years unknown and unnamed on Looe Reef, just off the main line of the Florida Keys. It was saved from anonymity in 1950 by a skin-diving family from Cleveland, Ohio.

Looe Reef was once a low, sandy island. Years ago, according to legend, a hermit lived there who spent his days salvaging silver from the wreck of a Spanish galleon. Dr. George M. Crile, Jr., and his wife, Jane, heard about the legend while on vacation in Florida and decided to investigate. Accompanied by their four children and a group of friends they rented a motor boat in Marathon and headed out across the sparkling waters of the Gulf of Mexico.

When the boat got to the reef the Crile party donned face plates and flippers and plunged into the clear, shallow water. A few minutes later one of the swimmers shouted excitedly that he had found a wreck. Rushing to join him the others looked below and found the sea floor strewn with oblong metal bars and twisted metal wreckage. Embedded in the coral bank was the remains of a huge anchor. Nearby they identified several cannon. Scattered among them were many coral-encrusted cannon balls.

With a rush of hope the Criles guessed that the metal bars might be silver. The coral encrustation was stained black, the color of silver sulphide. But to everyone's dismay the bars were far too heavy to lift to the deck of the boat. Their attempts to chip off a piece of metal for analysis also met with failure. On the far horizon black rain clouds warned them of an approaching storm. Taking a last despondent look at what they suspected was a fortune in silver the swimmers climbed back into their boat and headed for the safety of the Marathon harbor.

The Criles returned to the wreck the next day with a barge and a power winch for lifting the bars. The dawn was overcast and gusty winds whipped the sea into a froth. They knew better than to be out in such weather, but they were determined to bring back some of the bars. The second attempt was as unsuccessful as the first. The barge lurched and wallowed in the heavy seas. Time and again the ropes that were slipped around the heavy ingots were cut by the sharp coral banks. Storm warnings once again forced the Criles to leave Looe Reef. They reached Marathon just before a hurricane struck.

The treasure hunt had to be abandoned until Dr. Crile's next vacation. In the meantime he sent off a collection of coins and buttons to Mendel Peterson at the United States National Museum for identification. Peterson found them so interesting that he decided to join the treasure hunters on their next trip to Looe Reef. He learned two things about the wreck. One of the coins was a Swedish half-ore piece dated 1720. Since Scandanavian money would not likely be found in the wreckage of a Spanish galleon Peterson concluded that the wreck was of some other nationality. He also knew that the ship could not have been lost before 1720, the date on the coin.

The Crile family returned to Looe Reef seven months later in the warm, calm month of June. Their party had grown. The three boats that anchored over the wreck overflowed with fifteen adults and nine children. Among the newcomers were Ed and Marion Link aboard their trim white yawl *Blue Heron*. This was the Link's first adventure in underwater archaeology. The *Sea Diver* was not conceived until the following year.

The two other boats had been brought by the Criles from Marathon. One was the same clumsy barge used before. The other was a thirty-foot fishing boat named the *Little Whale*. On the deck were four air compressors and an assortment of diving gear, jet hoses, water pumps, crowbars, and winches.

The treasure fever of the previous summer had diminished slightly. Everyone had to admit that the historical data supplied by Peterson did not fit a Spanish ship. Morever, he had explained to them that silver was usually found in seventy-pound bars. It was never cast in ingots so massive that four men could not lift them. Final judgment was reserved, however, until one of the bars was finally hoisted to the deck of the barge. Dr. Crile ran to get the ship's compass. If the metal attracted the magnetic needle it was iron, if it did not it was probably silver. The needle trembled and dipped toward the bar, dashing all hopes of sudden wealth.

In the days that followed, the members of the expedition dived on the wreck site. The weather was ideal. The water was warm and so clear that objects could be seen clearly on the bottom, thirty-five feet below. The divers used Desco air masks, a tight-fitting face plate attached to a rubber hose. They were far more practical than Aqualungs for excavating in the shallow water of the reef. Air was supplied directly to the diver through his hose from a gasoline compressor on deck.

Both an airlift and a jet hose were used to excavate the wreck and recover historical artifacts. The airlift operated on the same principle as the suction tube used in the Grand Congloué excavation. A compressor on deck powered it with forty cubic feet of air a minute. As the air rose in the tube it sucked up sand and bits of coral and dug a great hole in the floor of the reef. At the surface the mixture of sand and water gushed geyserlike out of the tube and back into the sea. A strainer at the base of the tube caught anything larger than a grain of sand. While one diver directed the airlift another examined the strainer for bits of bone, broken glass, pottery, coins, and buttons.

At another part of the wreck a diver "excavated" with the jet hose. Water pumped through the hose from the boat above was ejected with such force that it cut away the sea floor layer by layer. The loosened sand and coral floated away with the tide.

Everyone had a job. The divers took turns, and when not in the water tended the air hoses of those below. The older Crile children acted as messengers, skin diving down to straighten hoses, bring equipment, and carry back material to the boats. In a short time even the amateurs learned to tell coral encrusted metal from ordinary coral by the presence of black iron oxide or silver sulphide. Also, anything straight or symmetrical came to look suspiciously man-made.

Ed Link devoted himself to the project of raising one of the twenty-five-hundred-pound cannon. The power winch on board the barge proved inadequate for the purpose, so in a few days he rigged up a system of blocks and tackles. Ropes were slung around a cannon, and slowly and carefully it was hauled

up level with the keel of the *Blue Heron.* Then the trim little
sailboat headed for Marathon, dragging the heavy cannon
through the swells of the Gulf stream.

As soon as the cannon was deposited on the shore Peterson
energetically attacked the inch-thick crust of coral with a
sledge hammer. As the rough coating fell away a raised pattern
was exposed on the smooth black surface of the gun barrel.
Peterson scrutinized the pattern and his face brightened with
recognition. The central figure was a crowned Tudor rose,
emblem of the English ruling house of Tudor. Above it was a
Maltese cross, the emblem of the Knights of St. John of Jeru-
salem and a military insignia used for many centuries. Next
to the cross was the broad arrow used to mark British Crown
property. At least one mystery had been solved. The wreck
had once been a vessel of the British Royal Navy. The same
arrow was later found on parts of the ship's rigging and on
the copper hoops of the powder barrels.

The emblems did more than identify the nationality of the
ship. They also helped to date it. The crowned rose went out
of use after the death of Queen Anne in 1714. An iron cannon
on board ship did not last much over thirty-five or forty years.
Adding thirty-five years to 1714 Peterson concluded that the
cannon was lost in the sea sometime before the year 1750.

In the meantime Peterson picked up other clues. The divers
brought up over a hundred cannon balls, most of them twelve
and six pounders, indicating that the ship was heavily armed.
The metal bars that had caused such excitement earlier were
identified as permanent iron ballast, cast to fit in the hull.
Since a cargo ship would not use permanent ballast Peterson
decided that their wreck was a warship, a man-of-war of the
frigate class.

Back in Washington Peterson began a search of British
naval documents. Checking through the Admiralty list of British ships lost in America during the eighteenth century he
came across the entry "February 5, 1744, *Looe,* 44 guns, Cap-

tain Ashby Utting, Commanding, lost in America." Further checking showed that the information fit perfectly. Until that moment it had not occurred to anyone that Looe Reef might have been named for its victim!

The Public Record Office in London turned up a letter written by Captain Utting, describing the last cruise of his ship. It had been sent from Port Royal, South Carolina, and dated February 14, 1744.

The letter stated that the H.M.S. *Looe,* a square-rigged, three-masted man-of-war, was one of four ships in a flotilla commanded by Captain Ashby Utting. England, still in possession of her American colonies, was at war with Spain. Captain Utting had been ordered to patrol the sea off the newly-founded colonies of Georgia and South Carolina during the summer months and to protect them from invasion by Spanish forces in Florida. In the winter, his orders were to cruise the Florida straits and stop any Spanish shipping between Havana, Cuba, and St. Augustine, Florida.

On the day before the tragedy Captain Utting had captured an important prize. Cruising a few miles off the coast of Cuba he spotted a strange sail and the *Looe* gave chase. He soon caught up with the vessel, which was named the *Snow,* and observed that it was flying a French flag. Something about the ship aroused the Captain's suspicions and he ordered an investigation. He was well advised in doing so. The "French" ship turned out to be a former English vessel engaged in Spanish business and in the employ of the king of Spain. Utting determined to escort the *Snow* personally to Charlestown.

It was 6:00 P.M. when Captain Utting again set sail. He took careful bearings and stayed on deck until he felt assured that the ships had passed the Doubleheaded Shot, a small key lying in the Florida straits. Then, convinced that he was out of all danger, he went below deck to rest. The night was foggy, and following Utting's instructions the crew threw out a three hundred-foot sounding line every half hour. At 1:00 A.M. the line failed to reach the bottom. Fifteen minutes later the sailing master looked overboard and was shocked to see that the ship was in breakers and heading straight for a reef one hundred feet ahead. The Captain was awakened and hurried on deck just as the *Looe* struck the reef. The pumps were started and Utting ordered the cannon thrown overboard in an effort to lighten the ship. The main topsail was hauled and the boats were ordered out. Three or four more heavy seas crushed the *Looe* against the reef and it settled heavily into the water on its port side. Alongside it the *Snow* suffered the same fate. All hands reached the comparative safety of the reef, but the only items that could be salvaged from the ships were some barrels of fresh water, twenty bags of bread, and six barrels of powder.

When daylight came, Captain Utting surveyed the situation. It looked desperate. The low, sandy island had no source of fresh water and at any moment an unusually large sea might wash right over their refuge. For the moment escape was impossible. The longboats were unable to carry even the 280 men of the *Looe,* and Utting was also responsible for the crew of the *Snow.* To make matters worse the sailors were in dread of attack by the savage Calusa Indians of the Florida Keys, whom they believed to be cannibals. As a result they were restless and on the verge of mutiny.

Utting resolved the situation with that amazing mixture of courage and audacity that has made the British navy famous. He spotted a small sloop far out on the horizon, and convinced that it was Spanish sent his marines out in a longboat to capture it. The following morning the sloop was seen coming back with the longboat in tow. The Spanish crew, seeing the longboat approach, had deserted the sloop and the British marines had boarded it without so much as a drop of blood being shed.

On Wednesday, February 8th, Utting embarked his men in the longboat and the Spanish sloop. Before setting sail he took gun powder and poured it over the part of the *Looe* that was still above water. Just before rowing back to the boats he set it afire. Even so he feared the Spaniards would spot the wreckage and salvage some of the guns and anchors.

Although Utting set his course for Providence in the Bahamas his sloop became separated from the boats during a stormy night. Despite the fact that the sloop was overloaded and a wind of any size would have capsized it the Captain safely made port in South Carolina on February 13th.

Utting was later court-martialed in England for the loss of the *Looe*. He was acquitted, when it was shown that the wreck had been caused by a strong and unknown current rather than by negligence or incompetence.

Leaving the Gulf of Mexico and traveling northward along the east coast of the United States we come to Yorktown, Virginia. Wandering down the quiet streets of this little Tidewater village it is hard to imagine a time when it resounded with the roar of cannon and the tramp of marching feet. Yet it was here that the armies of Washington and Lafayette surrounded the British forces, while the French fleet blockaded the York River and prevented their escape. On October 19, 1781, the commanding British General, Cornwallis, surrendered, thus ending the Revolutionary War and assuring the independence of the American colonies. It was a memorable day in the history of the United States.

The fact that the British had a small fleet in the York River that was destined never to leave might have been all but forgotten were it not for the fact that the oystermen of historic Yorktown complained bitterly of fouling their lines or breaking their tongs on underwater obstructions. The obstructions were the remains of Cornwallis' fleet.

In the summer of 1781 Lord Cornwallis had decided to move his headquarters from Williamsburg to a point nearer the sea. His hope was to unite his land and naval forces in anticipation of the arrival of a large British fleet. His choice of Yorktown seemed logical. The river in which he anchored

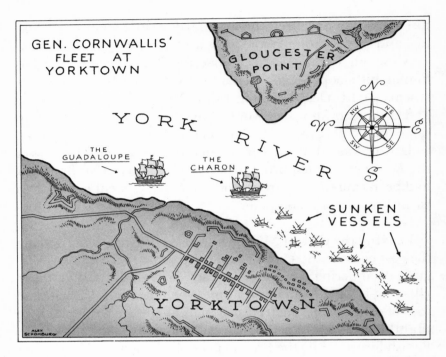

GEN. CORNWALLIS'
FLEET AT
YORKTOWN

GLOUCESTER POINT

YORK RIVER

THE GUADALOUPE

THE CHARON

SUNKEN VESSELS

YORKTOWN

ALEX SCHOMBURG

his small fleet was narrow. His shore batteries were sufficient to prevent the passage of enemy craft. Only later did he realize that he had unwittingly entered a trap.

The French forces allied with the colonists set up a blockade of the York River. Cornwallis ordered as many cannon as possible removed from the ships and taken ashore to strengthen the land batteries. By September 27th, when the actual march on Yorktown began, Cornwallis was desperate. His one attempt to break the blockade failed miserably. On October 9th the allies converged on Yorktown and fired the first shells. The following day the French battery succeeded in setting fire to the largest of the British ships, the forty-four-gun-ship *Charon*, and three of the smaller British transports. Cornwallis himself sank a large number of the less important vessels in order to form a breakwater and prevent the French fleet from sailing up the York River. Just before surrendering he scuttled the two largest remaining frigates, the twenty-eight-gun *Guadaloupe* and the twenty-four-gun *Fowey,* to prevent them being taken over by the enemy. The fighting came to an end with the signing of the articles of capitulation on October 19. Although the French navy took over the few British ships that were still intact and tried to patch up and refloat the more valuable of the sunken vessels a good many remained at the bottom of the York River.

They would have remained there except for the repeated complaints of the oystermen. Eventually these complaints reached the ears of officials of the Colonial National Historical Park of Yorktown and the Mariner's Museum of Newport News. In the summer of 1934 they co-sponsored an underwater investigation of the York River. Old records and maps were studied in an effort to establish the location of the sunken ships. The river near Yorktown was dragged and all obstructions were carefully plotted. Finally a diver in a helmet suit was lowered into the river. He worked off a barge moored in about forty feet of water. The articles that he recovered were deposited in a perforated metal basket or a clam shell bucket, and hoisted to the surface by a derrick and winch on the barge.

Two wrecks were found close together, almost completely disintegrated and buried in mud. The mud was removed with a fire hose and the diver took measurements. He concluded that they were vessels sixty to eighty feet in length.

Although the mud complicated the excavation it was responsible for the remarkable preservation of many perishable items. Wooden articles and fragments of rope were in excellent condition. Iron objects had not fared so well. Some of the cannon crumbled to pieces immediately after being exposed to the air. They had been cast of "gray iron," containing a network of flake graphite. During the 150 years of submersion the

iron had been completely corroded by the salt water, leaving
only the skeleton of graphite. Lead, copper, and pewter articles were well preserved, although the copper had a thick
patina. The many rum bottles were objects of beauty. The
years of contact with salt water had wrought a spectacular
change in the dark olive green glass, now covered with brilliantly iridescent scales reflecting all the colors of the rainbow.
Pottery and earthenware objects were in good condition,
though encrusted with oyster shells.

The valuable collection of eighteenth-century relics was di-
vided equally between the Colonial National Historical Park
and the Mariner's Museum, where it is now on exhibit. Although there was not sufficient evidence to enable the historians to identify the two wrecks by name everyone was well
pleased with the results of the excavation. Happiest of all were
the Yorktown oystermen.

There is an historic American ship that has been most per-
sistently sought but never discovered. This is the U.S.S. *Monitor,*
sometimes known as the "Yankee Cheesebox on a Raft." When
it made its debut on March 9, 1862, it was the answer to Presi-
dent Lincoln's prayers. Without it the Union might have lost
the Civil War.

Early in the conflict news reached the Union forces of an
invincible ironclad ship under construction by the Confed-
eracy. Thinking it best to be prepared Lincoln ordered the
construction of three experimental ironclads. One of them
was the pet project of a Swedish engineer named John Ericsson.

The ship designed by Ericsson was new to naval history. The
hull was almost all below the water line. On the deck was a
round tower, or turret, for the guns. The great innovation was
that the turret could be rotated and the guns fired in any direction. For months the inventor worked on his strange craft, hop-
ing desperately to have it ready before the Confederate forces

launched their ironclad monster, the *Merrimack*. The South won by one day.

On the morning of March 8, 1862, the *Merrimack* steamed toward the Union fleet at Hampton Roads, Virginia. It had been constructed from the burned-out hull of a Union frigate, left behind when the Union forces retreated from the Norfolk Navy Yard. The Confederate navy rebuilt it, adding on the deck a shed that was covered with heavy iron plates. The ten guns fired through ports protected by iron lids. An iron spike projected from the bow to puncture the ribs of wooden enemy ships.

The Union guns opened fire, but the cannon balls bounced harmlessly off the *Merrimack's* iron sides. Unfazed, the ship put on extra speed and headed straight for the Union frigate *Cumberland*. With a tearing shock it struck the *Cumberland* square amidships. At the same moment the guns fired a salvo of shells directly onto the frigate's decks. The *Cumberland* heeled over and water poured in through the huge hole in the side. After sinking the *Cumberland* the *Merrimack* attacked the *Congress* and set it afire. Then, since the *Merrimack* was running low on coal and ammunition, it steamed away.

The news reached Lincoln over the military telegraph. He called an emergency Cabinet meeting at six in the morning. Secretary of War Edwin McMasters Stanton expressed the fear of every member when he shouted, "Nothing can prevent her destroying every naval vessel and laying Washington in ashes. The war is lost. Nothing can save us but a miracle." Lincoln suggested that they all pray for one.

The miracle had already been accomplished by Ericsson. His ship, the *Monitor*, was on its way to the rescue. When the *Merrimack* appeared at six o'clock the morning of the 9th the *Monitor* sailed out to meet it. The two ironclads fought for hours. Each was unable to do any real damage to the other, and at last the *Merrimack* retreated. But the "Yankee Cheesebox" had saved the fleet of wooden frigates and turned the tide of war.

The two ships never met again. The Union forces captured the Norfolk Navy Yard two months later. Before they could take over the *Merrimack* it was destroyed by her own crew. On December 31st of the same year the *Monitor* was sunk in a storm off Cape Hatteras, North Carolina.

Someday, probably not too distant, divers will locate the grave of the *Monitor*. As the first of the ironclads it is of great historical significance. It also represents the closing chapter in the story of underwater archaeology. The battle at Hampton Roads signaled the end of wooden fighting ships and naval technology entered the modern era.

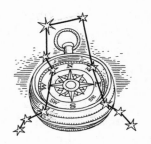

15

Shoals Ahead

At the close of the first Mahdia excavation in 1913 the noted art historian and archaeologist Salomon Reinach asserted that the bottom of the Mediterranean was the richest museum of antiquities in the world. He then added: "If technicians could only provide us with some means whereby we could personally explore its bed, how many sunken ships carrying masterpieces could we not discover!"

Reinach's wish has been granted. Since the days when his first poorly-equipped helmet divers struggled in the current and mud of the Tunisian sea floor there have been tremendous strides in man's conquest of the underwater depths. As Reinach correctly prophesied, countless sunken ships have been discovered. In 1953 divers of the *Calypso* surveyed the Aegean Sea, looking for wrecks on likely capes and reefs along the ancient trade routes. They found amphoras on almost every single dive! Some of them were isolated finds, but at least fifty deposits were large enough to indicate shipwrecks. They ranged in date from the Phoenicians to the late days of Rome.

Countless relics have been preserved that would long ago have fallen to dust had they been buried in the earth. This is particularly true for artifacts of plant or animal origin, such as the wood, leather, rope, and cloth found in the Sacred Well of Chichén Itzá and in the York River. The sea has protected them from generations of tramping feet and the tilling of the soil. Innumerable art masterpieces, such as the "Athlete" of

Antikýthēra and the "Thundering Zeus" of Artemísion, have
been protected from the greed and carelessness of men who
would have destroyed them out of ignorance or superstition.

These sunken ships have given us far more than art masterpieces. A preserved wreck is a slice of life that has been suddenly
petrified. Since the tragedy occurred at one particular moment
in the past everything found in the ship is contemporaneous.
One dated artifact is usually all that is necessary to relate the
ship to known history. Moreover, every item recovered from a
wrecked ship tells us something about the people who built
and sailed it. Artifacts peculiar to ships and seafaring reveal
little-known details of maritime life and technology. The types
of cargo found in merchant ships, such as that of Grand Congloué, add to our knowledge of ancient commerce. From them
we learn the origins and destinations of different exports and
imports. A warship, like the *Looe,* can be expected to yield information bearing on naval history. One single relic, such as
the astronomical computer found at Antikýthēra, has added
considerably to our understanding of Greek science.

The excavation of underwater shrines such as those at Lake
Amatitlán, Chichén Itzá, and Dzibilchaltun has given us new
insight into the ceremonial and religious life of the people who
made the offerings. In addition we can look with awe at an impressive array of art objects that were intended originally only
for the eyes of the gods.

Underwater archaeology has passed through its infancy: the
first stage of fortunate discoveries, amateurish attempts at salvage, and painfully-acquired experience. It has spread from its
birthplace in the Mediterranean to all of the seas and oceans of
the world and to many of the inland lakes and rivers. Now it is
ready to acquire the respectability of a mature science. In the
past relics were recovered for their artistic value alone. In the
future art masterpieces will still be recovered and put on display in museums, but only after every shred of information
has been gleaned from the excavation. In the future we can

expect universities to offer special courses in underwater archaeology in which advanced students can learn theory and practice simultaneously. There is already one underwater archaeological field school at the University of Florida and another at Leghorn, Italy. There will soon be more.

It is high time that underwater archaeologists were being trained. The sport of historical treasure hunting is getting out of hand. New underwater archaeological sites are being discovered at an amazing rate. Scarcely a month goes by without a notice in the press of a new underwater archaeological discovery somewhere in the world. As more and more divers don fins and Scuba apparatus and learn to recognize the underwater landmarks of the past the rate of discoveries will accelerate. There is great challenge as well as adventure in the watery world beyond the looking glass.

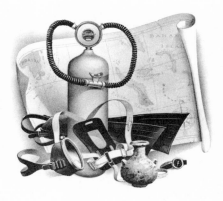

Appendices

Where To Explore Underwater

Now that you are prepared to explore underwater you will
want to know where to explore:

1. Consult an archaeologist or historian at your nearest university or museum. He may be able to supply you with valuable
   leads. If not, he can tell you where to find maps and charts
   showing the location of archaeological or historical sites on
   or near bodies of water.
2. Offer to coöperate with him if he plans an underwater excavation or a dry-land excavation of a site on or nearby a
   body of water.
3. Read up on the history and archaeology of your area and
   ask to study local archaeological and historical material.
   You will have to know exactly what to look for in order to
   recognize it underwater.
4. Don't limit yourself to archaeology and history. Make as
   many observations as possible on the underwater plant and
   animal life, geology, and mineralogy. Make collections and
   show them, along with your observations, to biologists and
   geologists at your nearest university or museum.
5. Don't be discouraged if you don't find anything right away.
   If the material were easy to find it probably would already
   be known.
6. Remember your responsibilities to science. When you make

an archaeological or historical discovery report it immediately to the nearest university or museum. In the meantime:

a. Do not disturb the site.
b. Make careful notes and sketches of what is there.
c. Mark the site with a buoy. A bottle anchored with a string or rope serves this purpose very well.
d. Estimate the depth with your depth gauge.
e. Do not tell its location to irresponsible friends, who might ransack the site without your knowledge.
f. Educate your fellow skin and Scuba divers in good underwater ethics. Help them to be conservation minded, to respect the fish and game laws, and to understand the scientific aspect of underwater archaeology. Encourage them to be explorers, not vandals.

7. Any body of water is a potential underwater archaeological site. Keep in mind the four different kinds of archaeological sites:

a. *Refuse sites.* In the western hemisphere these can be Indian, French colonial, Spanish colonial, British colonial or historical American. They will most likely be found near archaeological or historical sites on the shores of lakes, rivers, or the sea.
b. *Submerged settlements.* These will most likely be found in artificial lakes or dammed rivers or where the lake or sea level has risen greatly in recent years.
c. *Shrines.* The Indians of the Southeast and the Midwest United States and Latin America frequently considered springs to be sacred and cast offerings into them. Certain lakes were also considered to be sacred.
d. *Shipwrecks.* Historical shipwrecks can be found along either the Atlantic or Pacific coast, in the Gulf of Mexico, the Caribbean, and in the Great Lakes of the United States. Historical records are usually available in your local library.

8. Keep informed. Archaeological and historical discoveries are being made underwater in nearly every part of the globe. Many sites are now being excavated in the United States, in the Caribbean, the Mediterranean, Central and South America, Europe, and the Near East. Be on the lookout for newspaper and magazine articles describing the results of these and other recent underwater discoveries.
Good luck!

How To Explore Underwater

Those of you who want to explore for evidence of man's past in the underwater world must first prepare yourselves:

1. Learn to swim without swimming aids. Contrary to what you may have read elsewhere a competent knowledge of swimming is essential to skin and Scuba diving. Such items of equipment as mask, fins, snorkle, and Aqualung are wonderful swimming aids, but they may be lost or damaged unexpectedly while underwater. In such an event a knowledge of swimming may save your life.
2. Learn skin diving first.
   a. Buy your equipment from a good sporting-goods store and get the advice of an experienced diver. Cut-rate equipment is never a bargain.
   b. Practice where supervision is available.
   c. Learn the rules of first aid and life saving.
3. Learn Scuba diving from a qualified instructor.
   a. Co-educational courses in Scuba diving are offered at most Y.M.C.A.'s.
   b. Buy a good instruction manual and learn the facts of diving physiology.
   c. Become familiar with your equipment and its proper care and maintenance.

    d. Practice in a swimming pool before attempting to dive in lakes or in the ocean.

4. Get a thorough physical checkup from your family doctor.

5. Join a skin-diving club.

6. Use extreme caution when diving in unknown waters. It is best to have an adult with you, as or in addition to your diving buddy. Never underestimate the possibility of unforeseen dangers.

7. Never dive alone.

8. Check with your local hospital to learn where the nearest recompression chamber is located.

Bibliography

* *Suggests books for further reading*

ANDREWS, E. WYLLYS. "Dzibilchaltun: Lost City of the Maya," Washington D.C.: *National Geographic Magazine,* January, 1959.

BAKER, HENRY. "Sea Venture," Lynwood, California: *Skin Diver Magazine,* August, 1959.

BASS, GEORGE F. "A Bronze Age Shipwreck," Philadelphia, Pa.: *Expedition,* Winter, 1961.

* BEEBE, WILLIAM. *Half Mile Down,* New York: Duell, Sloan & Pearce, Inc., 1934.

BERT, PAUL, Tr. by M.A. and F.A. Hitchcock. *Barometric Pressure,* Columbus, Ohio: College Book Co., 1943.

BESSE, S.B. *U.S. Ironclad Monitor,* Newport News, Virginia: Mariner's Museum, 1936.

* BILLINGS, HENRY. *Man Under Water,* The Viking Press, Inc., 1955.

BORHEGYI, STEPHAN F. DE. "Aqualung Archaeology," New York: *Natural History,* March, 1958.

BORHEGYI, STEPHAN F. DE. "Underwater Archaeology in the Maya Highlands," New York: *Scientific American,* March, 1959.

BREUIL, ABBÉ H., Tr. by Mary E. Boyle. *Four Hundred Centuries of Cave Art,* Montignac, France, Dordogne: Centre D'Études et de Documentation Préhistoriques, 1952.

CARY, MAX. *Geographic Background of Greek and Roman History,* Oxford, England: Clarendon Press, 1949.

CASSON, L.S. "Sea Digging," Cincinnati, Ohio: *Archaeology,* Winter, 1953.

CASSON, L.S. "Trade in the Ancient World," New York: *Scientific American,* November, 1954.

CASSON, L.S. "More Sea Digging," Cincinnati, Ohio: *Archaeology,* Winter, 1957.

CASSON, L.S. *The Ancient Mariners,* New York: The Macmillan Co., 1959.

* CERAM, C.W. *Gods, Graves and Scholars,* New York: Alfred A. Knopf, Inc., 1952.

COSTEAU, J.Y. "Fish Men Discover a 2200-Year-Old Greek Ship," Washington, D.C.: *National Geographic Magazine,* January, 1954.

* COUSTEAU, J.Y., with DUMAS, FRÉDÉRIC. *The Silent World,* New York: Harper & Brothers, 1956.

* COUSTEAU, J.Y., and DUGAN, JAMES, (eds.). *Captain Cousteau's Underwater Treasury,* New York: Harper & Brothers, 1959.

BIBLIOGRAPHY

* CRILE, JANE and BARNEY. *Treasure Diving Holidays,* New York: The Viking Press, Inc., 1954.

DAVIS, SIR ROBERT H. *Deep Diving and Submarine Operations,* London, England: St. Catherine's Press, 1951.

* DE LATIL, PIERRE, and RIVOIRE, JEAN, Tr. by Edward Fitzgerald. *Man and the Underwater World,* New York G.P. Putnam's Sons, 1956.

DE SOLLA PRICE, DEREK J. "An Ancient Greek Computer," New York: *Scientific American,* June, 1959.

DIOLÉ, PHILIPPE. *The Undersea Adventure,* London, England: Sidgewick and Jackson, Ltd., 1953.

DIOLÉ, PHILIPPE. *4000 Years Under the Sea,* London, England: Sidgewick & Jackson, Ltd., 1954.

DONNELLY, IGNATIUS. *Atlantis: The Antediluvian World,* New York: Harper & Brothers, 1882.

* DUGAN, JAMES. *Man Under the Sea,* New York: Harper & Brothers, 1956.

* DUGAN, JAMES. *Undersea Explorer: Story of Captain Cousteau,* New York: Harper & Brothers, 1957.

Encyclopedia Americana, New York, Chicago, Washington, D.C.: Americana Corporation, 1957 edition.

END, EDGAR. "The Physiologic Effects of Increased Pressure," Berkeley, Stanford, and San Francisco: *Proceedings of the Sixth Pacific Science Congress,* Vol. VI, 1939.

FERGUSON, H.L. *Salvaging Revolutionary Relics from the York River,* Newport News, Virginia: Mariner's Museum, 1939.

GOGGIN, JOHN. "Underwater Archaeology, Its Nature and Limitations," Salt Lake City, Utah: *American Antiquity,* January, 1900.

HELLER, D.A. "Finding History Under the Sea," New York: *Natural History,* November, 1955.

HERMANN, PAUL. *Conquest by Man,* New York: Harper & Brothers, 1954.

HOWELLS, WILLIAM. *Back of History,* New York: Doubleday & Co., Inc., 1954.

JEWELL, DONALD P. "Fresh Water Archaeology," Mexico City: paper presented at the 58th Annual Meeting of the American Anthropological Association, 1959.

KARO, GEORGE. "Art Salvaged from the Sea," Cincinnati, Ohio: *Archaeology,* Winter, 1948.

* KENYON, LEY. *The Pocket Guide to the Undersea World,* New York: A.S. Barnes & Co., 1956.

LARSON, HOWARD E. *A History of Self-Contained Diving and Underwater Swimming,* Washington, D.C.: National Academy of Sciences, National Research Council Publ. 469, 1959.

* LINK, MARION. *Sea Diver,* New York: Holt, Rinehart and Winston, Inc., 1959.

LINK, MARION. "Exploring the Drowned City of Port Royal," Washington, D.C.: *National Geographic Magazine,* February, 1960.

MACKENDRICK, PAUL. *The Mute Stones Speak,* New York: St. Martin's Press, Inc., 1960.

MARDEN, LUIS. "Up from the Well of Time," Washington, D.C.: *National Geographic Magazine,* January, 1959.

MARINATOS, SPYRIDON. "Helice: Submerged Town of Classical Greece," Cincinnati, Ohio: *Archaeology,* Autumn, 1960.

* MASTERS, DAVID. *Epics of Salvage,* Boston: Little, Brown & Co., 1954.

* NESMITH, R.I. *Dig for Pirate Treasure,* New York: The Devin-Adair Co., 1958.

OUTHWAITE, LEONARD. *The Atlantic: A History of an Ocean,* New York: Coward-McCann, Inc., 1957.

PETERSON, MENDEL L. *History Under the Sea,* Washington, D.C.: Smithsonian Institution, 1954.

* POTTER, JOHN S., JR. *Treasure Divers of Vigo Bay,* New York: Doubleday & Co., Inc., 1958.

PRATT, FLETCHER. *Ordeal by Fire,* New York: William Sloane Associates, Inc., 1948.

ROBERTS, FRED M. *Basic Scuba,* Princeton, New Jersey: D. Van Nostrand Co., Inc., 1960.

SINGER, CHARLES, HOLMYARD, E. J., and HALL, A.R. (eds.). *A History of Technology,* Vols. I and II, London, England, New York: Oxford University Press, Inc., 1954.

* STIRLING, N.B. *Treasure Under the Sea,* New York: Doubleday & Co., Inc., 1957.

* TAILLIEZ, PHILIPPE. *To Hidden Depths,* New York: E.P. Dutton & Co., Inc., 1954.

* THOMPSON, EDWARD. *People of the Serpent,* New York: Houghton Mifflin Co., 1932.

THROCKMORTON, PETER. "Oldest Shipwreck Ever Found," Washington, D.C.: *National Geographic Magazine,* May, 1960.

TOZZER, A.M. *Chichén Itzá and Its Cenote of Sacrifice,* Cambridge, Mass.: Memoirs of the Peabody Museum, Vols. XI and XII, 1957.

VAN LOON, HENDRIK. *The Story of America,* New York: Liveright Publishing Corp., 1927.

WINBOLT, S.E. *Britain Under the Romans,* Harmondsworth Middlesex, England: Penguin Books, 1945.

Index

A

Acropolis, 79
Aegean Sea, 13, 14, 29, 52, 70, 157
Ahnlund, Professor, 90
air lift, 101, 147
Alaoui Museum, Bardo, Tunis, 65
Albemarle, Duke of, 132–134
Albenga, 89
Alexander the Great, 21, 26, 27, 58
Alinat, Lieutenant Jean, 66
American Antiquarian Society, 105, 111, 112
amphoras, 9–10, 51, 70–72, 76, 78, 89, 157
Andrews, Dr. E. Wyllys, 120
Anthéor, 8–11, 89
Antikythēra, 53–61, 62, 64, 65, 70, 80, 158
Aphrodite, 16
Apollo, 70
Aqualung, 30, 32, 34, 46, 66, 69, 91, 120, 124–125, 147, 163
Arabs, 19, 57
archaeological salvage, 44, 51
archaeology, underwater, 10–11, 40–49, 53–60, 61–68, 69–78, 79–91, 92–104, 105–120, 121–129, 130–140, 141–154, 162

Aristotle, 27
artifacts, 8–9, 53–54, 56–57, 59, 63–64, 66–67, 70, 74, 76, 82, 84–86, 87, 88, 89, 106–107, 113, 120, 125–129, 134, 137, 140, 144, 146–148, 153, 157–158
artificial air, 38
Artiglio II (salvage ship), 89
astrolabe, 19
astronomers, early, 13–14
astronomical computer, 57–58, 158
Athens, 16, 54, 56, 59, 64, 79, 87, 92–93, 95
"Athlete," 56, 59, 157
Atlantic Ocean, 14, 16, 17, 21, 92–94, 141
Atlantis, 92–94, 105
atmospheric pressure, 33–36
Aztecs, 93, 130, 131

B

Baehme, Admiral Jean, 61
Bahamas, 132, 134, 135, 136
Baltic Sea, 16, 19, 91
Barometric Pressure (book), 33
Bass, George, 86
bathygram, 50

169

H

Halley, Sir Edmund, 27–28
Hamilton, W.R., 80
Hansen, R.A., 36
Harvard University, 105, 118
Hatshepsut, Queen of Egypt, 12–13
Hawkins, J.A., 36
Helice, 94–96
helium, 38
helmet, 26, 28, 34
helmet-diving, 7, 33, 50, 66, 91, 153, 157
helmet suits, 7, 28–29, 30–31, 33, 34, 50, 62, 88, 116
Herculaneum, 62
Heurgon, Jacques, 9
Huout, Lieutenant Commander Georges, 21, 32
Hyde, James Hazen, 62
hydrogen, 38–39

I

Ice Age, 21–22, 83
Incas, 130–131
Institute of Jamaica, 101
Ionian Sea, 58, 71
Ionic marble columns, 61–63
Italian Institute of Ligurian Studies, 89

J

James II, King of England, 134–135

Jamestown, 142–143
Jefe Diós, 121–123, 129
Jourdan, Silvanus, 143–144

K

Karo, George, 88
Klingert, Otto, 28
Kondos, Captain Demetrios, 53–55, 59
Kythēra, 79

L

Lake Amatitlán, 121–129, 158
Lake Nemi, 81–83
Lallemand, Ferdinand, 76
Lamboglia, Professor Nino, 50, 89
Landa, Diego de, 110
Lassius, Caius, 9–10
Leghorn, Italy, 50, 159
Le Prieur, Commandant Yves, 30
Lincoln, Abraham, 154–155
Link, Ed, 50, 101–104, 136–137, 146–148
Littlehales, Bates, 120
Littleton, James, 102
Looe (ship), 148–151, 158
Looe Reef, 144–151

M

Macedonia, 58–59
McKee, Arthur, Jr., 136
Mahdia, 61–68, 69, 70, 75, 89, 157
Mahommet, 19
Marcus, 9–10
Marden, Luis, 120

Marinatos, Spyridon, 95–96
Mariner's Museum, Newport News, 153–154
Marius, 96
Marseille, 69, 71, 73, 76, 96
mask, 3, 5, 25, 40, 163
Mayan gods, 106–110, 114–120, 121–129
Mayans, 48, 93, 105–120, 121–129, 130
Médan, Henri, 76
Mediterranean Sea, 12–19, 51, 58, 64, 69, 90, 96, 157, 158, 163
Menachini, Basilio, 80
Mentor (ship), 80
Meritt, Benjamin Dean, 57
Merlin, Alfred, 61–65
Merrimack (ship), 155–156
Mexico, 48, 93, 105–120, 121–129, 132
Middle American Research Institute, Tulane University, 120
Monitor (ship), 154–156
Monmouth (ship), 139
Montespan, 83
mother-of-pearl, 22–24
Mount Hymettus, 64
Mount Vesuvius, 10
mud as preservative, 47, 53, 56, 62, 68, 153
Mussolini, 81

N

Naples, 72
National Geographic Society, 101, 120
National Maritime Museum, Stockholm, 91
National Museum, Athens, 56–57

navigation, early, 13–14
Navy Experimental Diving Unit, 91
Neptune, 16. *See also* Poseidon
Nicolas, 114–116
nitrogen, 35–38
nitrogen narcosis, 38. *See also* "rapture of the deep"
Nohl, Max Gene, 38
North Africa, 14, 19, 61, 64
North Star. *See* Polaris

O

Oscan alphabet, 9
oxygen, 29, 35, 38–39

P

Pacaya, 121, 124, 128
Pacific Islanders, 24
Parthenon, 79, 81
Peabody Museum, Harvard University, 105, 111, 112, 116, 118
pearls, 22–24
People of the Serpent, The (book), 114–115
Persian Gulf, 23, 24
Persians, 14–16
Peterson, Mendel, 102, 136–137, 140, 144, 145, 148
Philip II, King of Spain, 141–142
Philip V, King of Macedonia, 58
Phips, William, 133–136
Phoenicians, 13–16, 18, 24, 27, 48, 157
photography underwater, 41
Piccard, Auguste, 32

U

underwater archaeological field school, 159
underwater breathing apparatus, history of, 24–32
Underwater Mountain Climbing Club of Cannes, 9
underwater research ships, 48–50, 65–66, 69, 101, 136, 157
United States National Museum, 136, 145
United States Navy Standard Decompression Table, 36, 42
University Museum, University of Pennsylvania, 86
University of Florida, 159
University of Pennsylvania, 86
Ur, 23
Utting, Captain Ashby, 149–151

V

Van Den Ghein, Petrus, 140
Vasa, 90–91
Vernes, Jules, 29
Vigo Bay, 137–139

Vikings, 19, 90
Vinci, Leonardo da, 27

W

Walsh, Lieutenant Don, 32
water pressure, 34–39
Well of Sacrifice. *See* Sacred Well
Willm, Pierre, 21, 32
Wooley, Sir Charles Leonard, 23
Wreck Museum, Hamilton, Bermuda, 140

Y

Yax, Juan, 122
York River wrecks, 153–154, 157
Yorktown, 151
Ys, 94
Yucatán, 48, 105–120

Z

Zetterstrøm, Arne, 38–39

About the Author

Suzanne de Borhegyi received a B.A. degree in Biological Sciences from Ohio State University, and then began graduate studies in anthropology at the University of Arizona. While in Arizona she met and married a fellow anthropologist. Their interest in anthropology and archaeology has taken them to many fascinating and out-of-the-way places. They have lived in a Spanish village in New Mexico, worked with nutritional and medical field teams in mountain towns of Guatemala, and visited many archaeological ruins in the jungles of Central America. In Guatemala Mrs. de Borhegyi enrolled in San Carlos University for further courses in archaeology and anthropology.

SHIPS, SHOALS AND AMPHORAS grew out of research begun by her husband, who during the years 1956–60 directed the underwater excavations at Lake Amatitlán in Guatemala. To help him and to gain background for this book Mrs. de Borhegyi learned Scuba diving. Hundreds of artifacts were removed from the lake, and the local Indians believe that later droughts, rainstorms, and earthquakes were caused by this angering of the "old gods" who inhabit the lake.

Mrs. de Borhegyi now lives in Milwaukee with her four children and her husband, who is Director of the Milwaukee Public Museum. Their two older children are also enthusiastic skin divers.